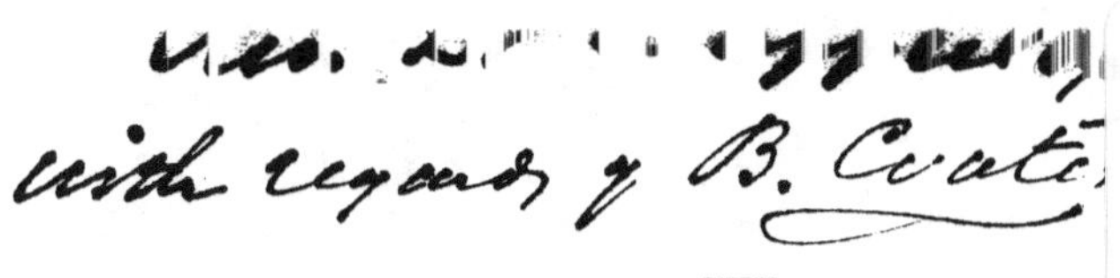

THE

POSITION OF CHRISTIANITY

IN THE

UNITED STATES,

IN ITS RELATIONS WITH OUR

POLITICAL INSTITUTIONS,

AND SPECIALLY WITH REFERENCE TO

RELIGIOUS INSTRUCTION IN THE PUBLIC SCHOOLS.

BY

STEPHEN COLWELL.

PHILADELPHIA:
LIPPINCOTT, GRAMBO & CO.
1854.

STEREOTYPED BY J. FAGAN. PRINTED BY T. K. AND P. G. COLLINS.

PREFACE.

EVERY year of our national existence brings increasing proof of the importance of the relations of Christianity with our political institutions. We began our history by extending Christian toleration to all: the value of that principle was evinced in our Colonial period. Such toleration as our fathers incorporated in our laws and constitutions having never before been tried, every year of experience under its operation becomes fraught with instruction to the philosopher, statesman, and Christian. It was, perhaps, difficult in the origin and outset of this experiment, to determine the exact bearings of such a policy on Christianity itself. Up to this time, our experience has shown not only the safety, but the wisdom of religious toleration. The whole Christian population of the country admire and approve it. It was not intended, however, in the establishment of this principle, that toleration should be an active policy, and Christianity a mere negative power. Christianity was not to be weakened, but made stronger by this proper exercise of its true spirit. It became important therefore from the beginning, and urgent that the true position of Christianity in the United States should be defined with that precision which, while it would, on the one hand, enlarge the scope of toleration and define its limits, would, on the other, clearly reveal the great highway of Christian effort and usefulness. This has never been adequately performed; and of late years the neglect has caused great embarrassment in many public functions, and great confusion of ideas among men of every class of opinion. Truth has lost ground, and is losing ground, for want of light on this subject.

Believing, as we do, that this is a Christian country, inhabited by a Christian people, that our political institutions are the work of a Christian people, designed to be administered in a Christian spirit, we hold that Christianity, instead of being stripped of its just power and influence in this land of toleration, imposes upon its friends the heaviest responsibilities, and expects to witness its greatest triumphs. Christianity here is not a negative, but a positive power. The problem is the starting point, and the path. Christianity, by toleration opened a door for all people to make their abode here: it is its function now to promote, by all the means within its compass, their highest interests here and hereafter.

We furnish the following pages with a view to dispel some of the doubts which hang over the subject, and with a hope of inviting others into a field of politico-religious literature which cannot be adequately explored but by many minds in many years.

We have endeavored to make it plain that the religious system of the United States is virtually Protestant: that the Christianity woven into the texture of our laws and political institutions cannot be other than Protestant. The Papal system, which holds that there can be no Christianity, no Christian worship, and no salvation, out of the Romish Church, regards our State constitutions as so many warrants for heresy, because they secure to every man the religious right to worship God as he pleases. The system of the United States recognizes one Christianity emanating from the Bible, but admits a diversity of worship and opinion if need be, to every individual man. Which of these irreconcilable systems shall constitute our permanent policy? The present system of Christianity for all, with liberty for all—unity of aim, with diversity of action — can only be maintained by a wise use of our present power and advantages. This Christian system, with its grand principle of toleration, must be maintained when needful at the polls, and vigilantly inculcated in the public schools.

PHILADELPHIA, *March* 25*th*, 1854.

CONTENTS.

SECTION I.

SECTION II.

SECTION III.

SECTION IV.

SECTION V.

SECTION VI.

SECTION VII.

THE POSITION OF CHRISTIANITY IN THE UNITED STATES.

SECTION I.

Reference to the position of Christianity before and during our Revolutionary period — Formation of our Political institutions. Religious liberty, toleration offered to all — Christian toleration — not merely toleration to Christians and others.

WHATEVER of religious intolerance survived our Colonial history was nearly worn out during the period of our struggle for independence. That was the united effort of men of various Christian denominations, all of whom appealed to God for the justice of their common cause and for that assistance which only Divine wisdom could give, and all of whom were grateful for that Divine favor which was so manifestly accorded. Their gratitude to the Great Giver of every good gift for the success of the effort was shown in very many unequivocal acts of thankfulness and praise. They felt that their success had imposed upon them not only cause of gratitude for the past, but heavy responsibilities for the future. They could not but realize that God in giving them the victory had made no distinction of persons nor of denominations. The blessing was common to all; it was becoming in all that their thanksgiving should be in unison and that the performance of the accruing duties of their position should be harmonious. It was in this spirit that our Revolutionary Fathers addressed themselves to the great task which lay before them. That task was to frame such political institutions as might secure to them, their posterity and the strangers from all the world who should seek a home in this favored land, all the liberty, comfort and happiness which individuals can enjoy consistently with the peace, welfare and order of an entire nation. What they had won together they meant to enjoy in common; they supposed that the exercise of the same virtues of self-denial, patience and trust in God which had given them victory in a struggle for existence, would secure to them all the blessings of peace, liberty and industry. They intended that the soil their efforts had redeemed should be a home to all the pilgrims of earth, driven by what cause soever from their native lands. None were excluded from the enjoyment of the benefits offered in a residence here, whatever their political or religious opinions, provided they submitted themselves to the few restraints of our laws and demeaned themselves in the spirit of our institutions. It was an asylum for the world which they established; it was a benevolent institution which they constructed and in which they offered to receive every human being who would enter and conform to its regulations. In proportion as these regulations were few in number and liberal in terms, was it necessary also that they should be firmly enforced. There could be no national liberty without law, and no peace without order. In offering a refuge to the suffering and to the discontented of all nations, they did not mean to surrender any of the advantages they had secured, nor to sacrifice any of the vital principles for which they had contended. They offered political liberty, but it was a liberty to be enjoyed under and in consistency with our legislation. They had no intention of surrendering their political institutions, in their form or spirit, to those who might prefer a despotic or monarchical form of government. There was a plain and necessary limit to their liberality; neither they nor their descendants nor successors were to be deprived of the benefits they had offered to others, under any pretence, or through any abuse of the privileges thus conferred. This reservation was no more than the right of self-preservation. They offered political freedom to all who might need the boon; but they did not offer the subversion of the very fabric they had reared for their own comfort and as an asylum to all others.

There was another limitation of their generosity equally vital. They were men of a Christian country; they reverenced the God of Christians; they acknowledged the revelation of his will contained in the Holy Scriptures; they derived the sanctions of their institutions, and the morality of their legislation and of their whole social system, from these Scriptures. They took themselves, and offered to all who came, religious liberty; they neither bound themselves nor others to any religious observance of the injunctions of God's word; but they neither permitted these Scriptures nor their Author to be blasphemed nor openly contemned, nor his worship to be disturbed. They neither established nor imposed any religious formality or doctrine as such, but they did not permit nor contemplate the substitution of any other code of morality than that which the Scriptures teach. They were fully aware of the debt which they owed to Christianity, and of the vital importance of its influence and teachings to modern civilization, and they could not abate one jot from the advantages thus to be gained. They constrained no man to be a Christian, nor to pretend to be one; but they held every citizen to acquiesce in the fact that Christianity was paramount to all other religions in the land, — that its morality was their morality, that its God was their God, and that it pervaded, controlled, and shaped, more or less, all their institutions and legislation.

It was in the very spirit of true Christianity that the hospitality and blessings of the United States were offered to all the world; all were invited to enjoy, and not to subvert. The Christian men of that day did not intend, in yielding to others political and religious freedom, to lessen their own privileges, nor to diminish the proper authority of Christianity in the land; they intended that the nation should continue to be a Christian nation, — that Christian morality should still pervade its legislation and social system, and that Christianity should continue to have a home here, at least, during the life of the nation. They did not place Christianity beneath nor over their political institutions: it was rather to be the atmosphere which they breathed who administered them; it was to be the source of their inspiration who sought to make them available for human advantage. These institutions and laws were to be the instruments of Christian men, for the good of the whole human family. The toleration, which was extended to all who chose to come within our borders, was Christian toleration. The Christianity of that day did not disfranchise itself; it did not admit that it was inferior to any other form of religion, nor did it concede that any other was its equal; it accepted no control from any other, nor placed itself under any dominion. It was no creature of the law, nor of our constitutions; it acknowledged them, and they acknowledged it. No other religion could, by any possibility, occupy the same relations to the people and their government as Christianity. It did not, therefore, accept toleration at the hands of the men who framed our system; they would have blushed at such a sentiment. Christianity was not a supplicant for their favor, and for a residence among them; they were Christian men, exercising Christian toleration towards others, and preparing for its continuance in all time to come. They could not, therefore, intend, in any degree, to lessen the benefits to be derived from this association with Christianity; they regarded it, indeed, as the very bulwark of their labors, and they believed that the blessings which would flow from them would be due more to the infusion of Christian sentiments than to any wisdom of their own.

The days of Church Establishments, or the union of Church and State, were then nearly numbered in this country. It was clearly perceived that Christianity claimed no secular office nor power. Its morality, as the morality of a Christian people, being already an ingredient of their common law, was to be carried by them still deeper into their legal and social systems. The government and laws were to be administered by Christian people: not by Christianity, not by a Church, nor by any Ecclesiastical authority of any kind. The only Christian control contemplated, was, the control of Christian men exercising that toleration which Christianity teaches. It was felt from the beginning that such institutions as were prepared for the United States would scarcely be safe in other than Christian hands, or in hands mainly controlled by Christian influences.

It could not have been otherwise than the intention of the founders of our Republic to perpetuate the Christianity to which they felt so deeply indebted and to the influences of which they chiefly looked for the continuance of the political institutions they had established. They could not but anticipate that any other than Christian hands would abuse the ample powers they had conferred upon officers and legislators, and they must have ardently desired that Christian activity and purity should keep pace with the growth and development of our population and material prosperity. These desires could not find any shape in the legal enactments of that period. They had launched the Republic and committed her to the Christian virtue and skill of those who were to be the navigators in after time. Much was to be done and learned in reference to the wise management of the great structure. The entire subject, if not wholly new, was presented in an entirely new aspect. One of the first charts demanded on this voyage is one which to this day has never been adequately sketched: that is, the precise position of Christianity in our political institutions. This subject should have been studied and carefully developed from the very origin of our system. The neglect has been so great and culpable, that errors in relation to it have taken deep hold of many truth-loving minds. It is now held by many such, though they may not actually so express their opinion, that Christianity is merely tolerated by our laws, and that it has no more connection with them than any other form of religion. It so happens, according to this opinion, that the people of this country are Christians, but their political institutions, they say, have nothing to do with that fact — being equally applicable to the government of Hindoos or Parsees. They exalt the idea of religious liberty into an absolute absurdity; and hold that a plea of the rights of conscience takes precedence of every other consideration. If this plea had any such interpretation in our system, it would overturn it when carried rigidly to its logical results. If a man can be protected in any opinion or any religious belief simply because it is the dictate of his conscience, he may set up doctrines subversive alike of government and of Christianity, and claim exemption from all accountability under the plea of religious liberty. Such is neither the spirit nor the fact of our institutions, which accord without limit or restraint neither political nor religious liberty.

Ours, from the beginning, was eminently a land of law. Just and necessary restraints are placed on every hand; no man is permitted to fix for himself the limits of his religious or of his political rights. All these are to a necessary extent subjects of law and public control. The utmost liberty is allowed which is consistent with public harmony and the good of the whole community.

No *reductio ad absurdum* can be more complete than that to which this claim of unlimited religious liberty is reducible; and the only reason it has not been long since driven from the minds of fair men, is because the topic being regarded as one of great delicacy is not often mentioned; and the argument is seldom pushed far enough to betray its utter weakness. The Christians of this country really tolerate only what is not inconsistent with their morality. They could not inhabit a country in which any obscene, profane, murderous or idolatrous rites might be practiced under their eyes in the name of any religion. As it is of the very spirit of our people to resist such an aggression as this upon their religious position, so it is of the very essence of our legislation to forbid it. We are a Christian people: our code of morals is Christian, our social system is Christian, and our civilization is Christian. This is our privilege and our pride. Shall we then directly or indirectly admit a principle, which, carried out, would prevent any national acknowledgment of God, and sever every relation between us as a people and Christianity?

Such an act of national skepticism or impiety was never for an instant contemplated by the founders of these republics. Any open, undisguised proposition to establish such a principle would now send a thrill of horror through the whole land, and bring upon its proposers the indignation of an entire population.

We are not a nation of Christians; but this is a Christian nation. Christianity has all the authority and control over our legislation, our institutions and their administrations, which, according to its true spirit, it can or ever will claim, — that which is exercised through the wisdom, energy, and influence of individual Christians. Will the Christians of this country abdicate this right, and concede the principle that heathens, idolators, or Buddhists are entitled to an equal participation in all the benefits of our government?

SECTION II.

Constitution of the United States — Its relations with Christianity. Oaths of Office — Religious tests and establishments.

CERTAIN provisions of the Constitution of the United States are sometimes cited in support of the position that the instrument itself does not, in any manner, recognize Christianity, and that the spirit of our political institutions is adverse to any such recognition. Let us examine whether these provisions are not, in fact, in perfect harmony with the principles for which we contend. The clause to which we shall first refer is that which requires that all the officers, "both of the United States and of the several States, shall be bound by oath or affirmation to support this constitution. But no religious test shall ever be required, as a qualification to any office or public trust under the United States."

The nature of official and judicial oaths and affirmations in this country is so well known that we need only say that such oaths and affirmations are directly or impliedly, an appeal to the Supreme Being, or an invocation of God to be witness of our sincerity, or of the truth of our averments. We need not argue or prove that this God, to whom all our public officers appeal, or whom they solemnly invoke, is the God of Christianity. No man, so far as we know, has been hardy enough to deny this; such a denial would shock the moral sense of the whole country. What, then, is the purport of this clause? It is simply this, that this very Constitution, which has been supposed by some to repudiate Christianity, does not commit itself, either for the interpretation of its intent, or the administration of its provisions, to any officers, judicial, legislative, or executive, until they have first sworn or promised before God to support it.

So far, therefore, from discarding Christianity and disowning God, the framers of this great Charter made an appeal to the Christian's God, an indispensable preliminary to exercising any high office in a State or in the nation. Before taking this oath no man could assume authority under this Constitution; it was the bond of fidelity, it was made a public security for the faithful discharge of official duties, and for the proper administration of the Constitution itself. Upon this bond, placed among the provisions of the Constitution by men representing a Christian community, the life and working of the instrument was rested. They committed it to the charge of posterity only on condition of their solemnly declaring before God that they would support it. When the true nature of an oath or an affirmation before God is considered, this clause of the Constitution is fraught with a significancy so pregnant that we can well understand why it was thought needful to restrict its meaning by the provision which follows.

The restriction, however important, and we add proper, leaves a force and meaning to the clause large and strong enough to cover every Christian claim. It leaves the administration of the Constitution only to those who shall promise before God to maintain it inviolate. As members of a Christian community they no doubt felt they could not do less, and they knew they could not do more. They exacted the highest obligation of fidelity known to Christians. They put the Christian seal upon the Instrument, that it might never be violated so long as Christian obligations should be the highest known to the people.

But these were men of toleration. They had seen and heard and known enough of religious tests and establishments to make them irreconcilable enemies of all intolerance and religious tyranny. They were framing political institutions intended to afford the largest civil and religious liberty consistent with public order and good government. They prescribed to all an oath — a promise before God, to every man, before he could lay an official hand upon the Constitution; but they forbade any "religious test to be required as a qualification to office." If this provision had stood alone in the Instrument, no oath could have been imposed upon those accepting office: but coming as a limitation of the previous clause, its import is not only clear, but in perfect consistency with the whole spirit of the Constitution and its authors. No man was permitted to accept of an office without a virtual acknowledgment of God, but no religious test was ever to be required; that is, among the numberless and conflicting religious opinions no distinction was ever to be made. The officer is required to make the oath or affirmation, but in no other respect is his religious belief to be brought in question. It was needful that this restriction should be broad enough to shut out all possibility of its being evaded by sectarian ascendency. The Constitution makes therefore no distinction, except that between those who are willing before God to swear or affirm, and those who may, from religious scruples, refuse either to swear or affirm. Such as thus refuse cannot take office under it. All others, whatsoever their religious opinions, may take official station, without inquiry into their sincerity or consistency in assuming this solemn engagement. The framers of the Constitution gave it therefore the broadest possible basis consistent with the fact, that it recognized the Christian's God, and was thereafter to be ever administered by men acknowledging Him as the Supreme Being.

The Christian nation which adopted this Constitution invited the people of every country to come and live under it; but in so doing they did not abdicate their Christian ascendency nor proclaim that their institutions were purged of the Christian element. They avowed toleration, and not infidelity, as their great principle. They said to all the persecuted and suffering throughout the world, Come and dwell with us and you may enjoy manifold advantages and immunities. We are a Christian people, our institutions are constructed with reference to Christianity, and are intended to be administered under its light and influences; it teaches us to offer you the largest Christian liberty ever enjoyed by a civilized people—

the largest possible consistent with the existence of Christianity itself. It is the light of Christianity which enables us to offer this boon to all people, but while we make the boon great we can never permit the light to be extinguished which disposes and enables us to confer this signal favor. The right of private judgment will be accorded to all who come to our shores to the utmost extent consistent with the continued existence and comfortable enjoyment of our present Christianity. In offering these advantages of civil and religious liberty to the people of every creed and nation, they, our ancestors, did not concede any principle of the great work they had just finished; they did not propose to take down their fabric or fashion it to the taste of all who might take refuge within its walls; they did not propose to place the existence of Christianity and Christian civilization in our land at the mercy of those who should make their abode with us; they intended to extend a real Christian toleration to all people, but they did not mean that the idolators or pagans who might come among us should be regarded in their turn as tolerating Christians. They intended that it should remain a Christian land, and that the glory of its toleration should continue to be ascribed to its true origin, Christianity.

In his Commentaries on the Constitution, Judge Story (vol. 3. § 1841), speaking of this clause, remarks, "It is not introduced merely for the purpose of satisfying the scruples of many respectable persons who feel an invincible repugnance to any religious test or affirmation. It had a higher object: to cut off forever every pretence of any alliance between

Church and State in the National Government." It was not intended to cut off or put any slight upon Christianity. It was the deliberate severance of Church and State, and a declaration, that according to their views, there neither was nor should be any such alliance. They admitted no other connection between Church and State than what existed between the people and their government. The Constitution was to be maintained, upheld and administered by, as its makers trusted, a Christian people. They did not commit the perpetuation of Christianity to the Constitution, but they committed the Constitution, as a sacred trust, to the Christian people who were to be its protectors and administrators; and having provided against sectarian partialities, they never believed it would be safe in any other hands than those under Christian influences. This is plain from innumerable facts and considerations which appear in all our history as a people.

It would have been easy to declare, in so many words, that Christianity should have no precedence in our system over any other religion; to have abolished official and judicial oaths, to have repealed all enactments in reference to the Lord's day, to have prohibited the appointment of Chaplains or the proclamation of Thanksgivings; and finally, by one sweeping statute, to have severed the existing connection between our common law and Christianity, thus legalizing blasphemy and abolishing our code of morals, the basis of Christian civilization. So far from this, whatever be our short-comings as a religious people, every page of our history reveals the great fact that as a nation we acknowledge the God of the Bible and no other.

We revert again to the Constitution of the United States. The first article of the amendments provides that, "Congress shall make no law respecting an establishment of religion, or prohibiting the free exercise thereof." This is an explicit prohibition of any union of Church and State. The theory of the framers of this Instrument was, that there need not be and should not be any union of our ecclesiastical with our political institutions; that the relations of Government with Christianity should be through individuals and not through Churches; and that the bearings of Christianity on the legislation and administration of Government should be that which is effected by the influences and efforts of Christian citizens. They not only offered religious toleration to all who differed from them in opinion, but they gave them a voice and a vote in reference to the mode in which that Christian toleration should be exercised. They not only extended toleration to those of different faith, but they gave these securities to those who might avail themselves of it, providing however, that if the tolerated party should become dominant, no law should ever be made prohibiting the free exercise of religion. They agree not to establish Christianity as a religion, but expressly provide that no law shall ever prohibit its free exercise. Any other religion inconsistent with Christianity may be prohibited, but the Christion religion is declared to be out of the reach of Congressional interference. Legislation may promote the interests of religion by any measures not inconsistent with toleration, but it cannot destroy them. Congress has power, and with that power devolves the duty to provide for the general welfare of the United States; so far as it can, it should promote the interests of religion as one of the most efficient means of promoting the general welfare: its powers in this respect are only limited by what is due to the right of private judgment by the provisions of the Constitution itself and by what is due to that Christian toleration which is of the essence of our institutions.

SECTION III.

Citations from Story's Commentaries on the Constitution of the United States. Chaplains for Army and Navy, — De Tocqueville, Alex. Hamilton.

THIS subject is discussed at some length in his Commentaries on the Constitution by Judge Story, one of the ablest of our writers on jurisprudence and constitutional law, long a judge of the Supreme Court of the United States, of high repute for learning and sound opinions. We take from his remarks on the clause of the Constitution just quoted, a few passages which sustain our views.

"It is impossible for those who believe in the truth of Christianity as a divine revelation to doubt that it is the especial duty of government to foster and encourage it among all the citizens and subjects. This is a point wholly distinct from that of the right of private judgment in matters of religion and of the freedom of public worship according to the dictates of one's conscience." (vol. 3, page 723, § 1865.)

"Now there will probably be found few persons in this or any other Christian country who would deliberately contend that it was unreasonable or unjust to foster and encourage the Christian religion generally as a matter of sound policy as well as of revealed truth. In fact, every American colony, from its foundation down to the Revolution, with the exception of Rhode Island (if indeed that State be an exception), did openly by the whole course of its laws and institutions, sustain in some form the Christian religion; and almost invariably gave a peculiar sanction to some of its fundamental doctrines. And this has continued to be the case in some of the States down to the present period, without the slightest suspicion that it was against the principles of public law or republican liberty. Indeed, in a republic there would seem to be a peculiar propriety in viewing the Christian religion as the great basis on which it must rest for its support and permanence, if it be what it has ever been deemed by its truest friends to be, the religion of liberty." (*Ibid.* page 724, § 1867.)

"Probably at the time of the adoption of the Constitution, and of the amendment to it now under consideration, the general, if not the universal sentiment in America was, that Christianity ought to receive encouragement from the State, so far as was not incompatible with the rights of conscience and the freedom of religious worship. An attempt to level all religions, and to make it a matter of State policy to hold all in utter indifference, would have created universal disapprobation, if not universal indignation."* (*Ibid.* 726, § 1868.)

---

* Lloyd's Debates, 195, 196.

"It yet remains a problem to be solved in human affairs, whether any free government can be permanent, where the public worship of God and the support of religion constitute no part of the policy or duty of the State, in any assignable shape. The future experience of Christendom, and chiefly of the American States, must settle this problem, as yet new in the history of the world, abundant as it has been in experiments in the theory of government." (*Ibid.* § 1869.)

"But the duty of supporting religion, and especially the Christian religion, is very different from the right to force the conscience of other men, or to punish them for worshipping God in the manner which they believe their accountability to him requires." * * "The rights of conscience are indeed beyond the just reach of any human power. They are given by God, and cannot be encroached upon by human authority without a criminal disobedience of the precepts of natural as well as of revealed religion." (*Ibid.* § 1870.)

"The real object of the amendment was not to countenance, much less to advance Mahometanism, or Judaism, or infidelity, by prostrating Christianity; but to exclude all rivalry among Christian sects, and to prevent any national ecclesiastical establishment which should give to an hierarchy the exclusive patronage of the national government. It thus cut off the means of religious persecution (the vice and pest of former ages), and of the subversion of the rights of conscience in matters of religion, which had been trampled upon almost from the days of the Apostles to the present age." (*Ibid.* § 1871.)

"It was under a solemn consciousness of the dangers from ecclesiastical ambition, the bigotry of spiritual pride, and the intolerance of sects, thus exemplified in our domestic as well as in foreign annals, that it was deemed advisable to exclude from the national government all power to act upon the subject." . . . . . . "Thus the whole power over the subject of religion is left exclusively to the State governments, to be acted on according to their own sense of justice and the State Constitutions; and the Catholic and the Protestant, the Calvinist and the Arminian, the Jew and the Infidel, may sit down at the common table of the national councils without any inquisition into their faith or mode of worship." (*Ibid.* p. 730, § 1873.)

It must be remarked, that the last paragraph refers to the dangers of "ecclesiastical ambition," and of course to churches or bodies of men organized as such. The only power which Congress has over the subject is that which relates to the welfare of the country in its moral and religious aspects, and that under the limitations we have already mentioned. Congress has no power over the subject as it relates to any church or ecclesiastical body. It can recognize the fact that this is a Christian country, it can promote the welfare of its Christian citizens as such, it can impose no form of worship, it can force no man's conscience, but it can seize many occasions of favoring the interests of Christianity; it can, so long as a majority desire it, by its own Chaplain, ask the blessing of God upon its deliberations, but it could not enforce the presence of any member who objected to this act of worship. In fact, the members of Congress have only such powers in relation to religion as belong to them individually and such as have not been excluded from their consideration by the Constitution itself. The power thus left to Congress, though exceedingly restricted, would be large if exercised for the good of the whole nation in the enlarged spirit of that Christianity which requires men to love others as they love themselves. Under this great law the Congress of the United States has power to promote the general welfare to the full extent of all their wisdom and skill without trenching on any religious dogma in a way to excite jealousy or apprehension even in the most sensitive.

The labor of the country, and of course the destiny and welfare of laborers, is obviously within the reach of the national legislature. Christianity teaches that the laborer is worthy of his hire, and it imposes upon those who have the power, the duty of not only shielding them from harm and imposition, but of promoting their interests in every way which may be consistent with justice and mercy and not inconsistent with the interests of society at large. So Congress can promote the interests of Christianity as a means of ensuring national well-being, provided the principle of toleration be not violated. It would undoubtedly be right in Congress to view the whole subject of the welfare of the people for whom it legislates in the light of Christianity. It may not take any notice of the homage which men owe to God, but it cannot wholly overlook the duties which men owe to one another. It may restrain selfishness and promote within the range of its action, general well-being, though it cannot enforce any religious tenet or form of doctrine.

The disposition of the National Legislature to act in accordance with these principles was shown from the earliest period of their action. A Chaplain was chosen to open their meetings with prayer and to preach on the Lord's day. Chaplains were by law provided for in the Army and Navy. In the Act for the better government of the Navy of the United States, is the following clause: "The commanders of all ships and vessels in the Navy having a Chaplain on board, shall take care that Divine service be performed in a solemn and reverent manner twice a day, a sermon preached on Sunday, unless bad weather or other extraordinary accidents prevent it; and that they cause as many of the ship's company as can be spared from duty, to attend every performance of the worship of Almighty God." (1 Story's Laws U. S. 761.)

In the Act establishing rules and regulations for the Army of the United States, is the following clause: "It is earnestly recommended to all officers and soldiers diligently to attend Divine service." This is followed by severe penalties for improper behavior at any place of Divine worship; and by another clause visiting with penalties any officer or soldier "who shall use any profane oath or execration;" and by another, providing penalties against "every Chaplain commissioned in the Army or Armies of the United States, who shall absent himself from the duties assigned him." (2 Story's Laws U. S. 992.)

We might add to these many other proofs of Congressional acknowledgment of Christianity, but we shall advert further only to a joint resolution of both Houses on the occasion of the War of 1812. "It being a duty peculiarly incumbent in a time of public calamity humbly and devoutly to acknowledge our dependence on Almighty God and to implore His aid and protection, therefore resolved, that a joint committee of both Houses wait on the President and request him to recommend a day of public humiliation and prayer, to be observed by the people of the United States with religious solemnity and the offering of fervent supplications to Almighty God for the safety of these States and the speedy restoration of peace." Upon occasion of the restoration of peace in 1815, Congress again united in recommending the appointment of a day of Thanksgiving. President Madison acceded to both these legislative requests, and the days were appointed and observed. Various Presidents have since then made similar appointments. It is therefore abundantly evident, that this Nation, both in its Legislative and Executive capacity, acknowledges God and the Revelation of His will in Christianity.

This national homage to God has not failed to strike the notice of observing strangers, who attentively regard the working of our political institutions. One of the most profound Statesmen who has visited our country, remarks: "There is no country in the whole world in which the Christian religion retains a greater influence over the souls of men than in America; and there can be no greater proof of its utility and conformity to human nature, than that its influence is most powerfully exercised over the most enlightened and free nation of the earth." . . . . . . "In the United States religion exercises but little influence upon the laws, and upon the details of public opinion; but it directs the manners of the community, and by regulating domestic life it regulates the State." . . . "Christianity, therefore, reigns without any obstacle, by universal consent; the consequence is, that every principle of the moral world is fixed and determinate, although the political world is abandoned to the debates and experiments of men." . . . . . . "I cannot say that all Americans have a sincere faith in their religion, for who can search the human heart? but I am certain that they hold it to be indispensable to the maintenance of republican institutions. This opinion is not peculiar to a class of citizens or a party, but it belongs to the whole nation and to every rank of society." . . . . . . "The Americans combine the notion of Christianity and of liberty, so intimately in their minds, that it is impossible to make them conceive the one without the other." . . . . "Such are the opinions of Americans; and if any hold that the religious spirit which I admire is the thing most amiss in America, and that the only element wanting to the freedom and happiness of the human race is to believe in some blind cosmogony, &c., I can only reply that those who hold this language have never been in America, and that they have never seen a religious or free nation." (De Tocqueville, American Institutions, chap. xvii.)

We might readily multiply such testimonies to the Christian character of our institutions. We might also have quoted largely from the writings and speeches of the very Fathers of our country, the authors of these institutions; but this would have carried us into a field far too wide for the limits of this essay. It is worthy of mention, however, that when the infidelity which characterized the French Revolution of the last century had spread its poisonous influences even to our shores, it became a source of serious disquietude to the good men of that day, and especially to our Revolutionary Fathers then surviving. Hamilton, in a letter to Bayard, dated in 1802, proposes the formation of a National Society, under the title of "Christian Constitutional Society," having for its object, "1st, The support of the Christian religion;" "2nd, The support of the Constitution of the United States." (Hamilton's Works, vol. vi. p. 542.)

SECTION IV.

The early Constitutions of the American States on the subject of Christianity and Religious liberty.

The Constitutions of many of the original thirteen States contained a very marked acknowledgment of Christianity. Connecticut and Rhode Island continued under the government of the ancient Charters, of Puritan origin and founded on Christian principles. The States of New Hampshire, Massachusetts, and New Jersey, by their Constitutions, expressly recognized Protestant Christianity, whilst they expressly provide for the privilege of worshipping God according to the dictates of conscience. That of New Hampshire had these provisions, "That morality and piety rightly grounded on evangelical principles would give the best and greatest security to government, and would lay on the hearts of men the strongest obligations to due subjection."

The Constitution of Massachusetts has the following: "That as the happiness of a people, and the good order and preservation of civil government, essentially depend upon piety, religion, and morality; and as these cannot be generally diffused through a community but by the institution of the public worship of God and of public instruction in piety, religion and morality, therefore" &c. Then follows a provision for the establishment and maintenance of public worship, and for the maintenance of "public Protestant teachers of piety, religion and morality." It prescribes also that the person chosen Governor, Lieutenant Governor, Senator or Representative, shall subscribe a solemn profession, "that he believes the Christian religion, and has a firm persuasion of its truth."

The first Constitution of New York is dated in 1777. It strongly guarded the rights of conscience and religious worship. It excluded the Clergy from public offices of a secular nature, on the express ground, that by their profession they were dedicated to the service of God and to the cure of souls, and ought not to be diverted from the great duties of their functions.

The first Constitution of New Jersey is dated in 1776. The 18th section provides, "That no person shall ever within this colony be deprived of the inestimable privilege of worshipping God in a manner agreeable to the dictates of his own conscience; nor be compelled to attend any place of worship, nor to pay tithes, taxes, &c., to build churches or maintain ministers — also, that there shall be no establishment of any one religious sect—that no Protestant shall be denied any civil right."

The first Constitution of Pennsylvania, made in the year 1776, requires each member of the Legislature to make this solemn declaration: "I do believe in one God, the Creator and Governor of the Universe, the Rewarder of the good and the Punisher of the wicked, and I do acknowledge the Scriptures of the Old and New Testament to be given by Divine inspiration."

The Constitution of Delaware, made in 1776, requires all officers and members of the Legislature to subscribe the following declaration: "I do profess faith in God the Father and in Jesus Christ his only Son and the Holy Ghost, one God, blessed forevermore; and I do acknowledge the Holy Scriptures of the Old and New Testament to be given by Divine inspiration."

The Constitution of Maryland, made in 1776, empowers the Legislature to lay a general tax for the support of the Christian religion. No tests are permitted, except, an oath of office, an oath of allegiance, and "a declaration of belief in the Christian religion."

In Virginia, previous to our National Independence, religion was established by law. No mention was made of the subject in a Constitution drawn up under the influence of, if not by, Jefferson himself.

The Constitution of North Carolina, adopted in 1776, provides, "That no person who should deny the being of a God, or the truth of the Protestant religion, or the Divine authority of either the Old or the New Testament, or who should hold religious principles incompatible with the freedom or safety of the State, should be capable of holding any office or place of trust in the civil government of the State."

The Constitution of South Carolina, made in 1788, expressly ordains, that "the Christian religion be deemed and is hereby constituted and declared to be, the established religion of the land." It excludes from the Legislature, and from the office of Governor and Lieutenant Governor, and from the privy council, all who are not Protestants. It provides for Protestant religious worship and the incorporation of congregations under the description of "Societies of Christian Protestants," prescribing a strictly orthodox formula as the condition of incorporation. It contains also the form of a declaration of very stringent nature to be made and subscribed by every Minister before he can enter upon the pastoral office.

The Constitution of Georgia, made in 1777, prescribes that "all members of the House of Assembly shall be of the Protestant religion."

These State Constitutions were formed before the Constitution of the United States. The principles of toleration were at work, but had not sufficiently liberalized the minds of the Statesmen who drew up these early Charters. It was not until after the termination of the War and the formation of the National Constitution, that the subject of toleration began to be understood. But even then there was a confusion of ideas on the whole subject of the relation of our political institutions with Christianity, which made it a *desideratum* that some competent hand should draw up a bold outline of these relations, which could be readily comprehended and made the basis thereafter of Constitutional and Legislative action. This has never yet been done, and the cause of truth and Christianity has suffered by the omission more than can be easily estimated. Not so much, however, in reference to the duty of toleration, as in a clear perception of the position and bearings of Christianity after full toleration had been accorded.

In all the States, we believe, the distinctions made in favor of Protestantism have been removed and the rights of conscience expressly acknowledged and secured. That is, the right to worship God according to his own tenets or views is guaranteed to every citizen. No rights are by these provisions guaranteed to infidels or unbelievers; they have other rights as citizens which are secured by Constitutions and laws, but they can claim no privileges of any kind under a guarantee of *religious* liberty. They are in fact fully tolerated by the spirit of our institutions so long as their unbelief is not in any manner exerted against Christianity, either by profanity, blasphemy or by writing or speaking maliciously against religion.

"Rights of conscience are religious rights, that is, the right to entertain and utter religious opinions, and to enjoy public religious worship. This expression, in its widest acceptation, cannot include irreligion,—opinions contrary to the nature of religion, subversive of the reverence, love and service due to God, of virtue, morality and good manners." (Dr. Baird's Religions in America, book iii. chap. 9.)

SECTION V.

THE EXISTING CONSTITUTIONS OF THE SEVERAL STATES.

Maine.

To save the trouble of reference, we proceed to give some of the leading provisions of the existing State Constitutions in regard to religion. Art. I. sect. 3. "All men have a natural and inalienable right to worship Almighty God according to the dictates of their own consciences, and no one shall be hurt, molested or restrained in his person, liberty or estate, for worshipping God in the manner and season most agreeable to the dictates of his own conscience, nor for his religious professions or sentiments, provided he does not disturb the public peace, nor obstruct others in their religious worship; and all persons demeaning themselves peaceably, as good members of the State, shall be equally under the protection of the laws, and no subordination nor preference of any one sect or denomination to another shall ever be established by law, nor shall any religious test be required as a qualification of any office under this State."

New Hampshire.

After a provision nearly in the same words as that of Maine, the Constitution of New Hampshire has in Part I. sect. 6, this clause: "As morality and piety, rightly grounded on evangelical principles, will give the best and greatest security to government, and will lay in the hearts of men the strongest obligations to due subjection," &c.: then follows a provision to encourage the public worship of God and authority to the Legislature to incorporate religious societies, &c.

VERMONT.

To a provision nearly identical with that of Maine, Vermont adds, "Nevertheless, every sect or denomination of Christians ought to observe the Sabbath or Lord's day, and keep up some sort of religious worship which to them shall seem most agreeable to the revealed will of God." (Chap. I. sect. 3.)

MASSACHUSETTS.

Part I. sect. 2. "It is the right as well as the duty of all men in society publicly and at stated seasons to worship the Supreme Being, the Great Creator and Preserver of the Universe. And no subject shall be hurt, molested or restrained in his person, liberty or estate, for worshipping God in the manner and seasons most agreeable to the dictates of his conscience; or for his religious profession or sentiments, provided he does not disturb the public peace or obstruct others in their religious worship."

3. "As the happiness of a people and the good order and preservation of civil government, essentially depend upon piety, religion and morality, and as these cannot be generally diffused throughout the community but by the institution of a public worship of God and of public institutions of piety, religion and morality, therefore to promote their happiness and to secure the good order and preservation of their government," the Legislature is authorized to make provision "for such public worship and such institutions," &c., "in all cases where such provision shall not be made voluntarily." It is provided that every man who contributes under a law of the State to the support of religion, "may designate to what denomination his tax shall be applied."

Rhode Island.

"We, the people of Rhode Island, grateful to Almighty God for the civil and religious liberty He hath so long permitted us to enjoy, and looking to Him for a blessing upon our endeavors to secure and transmit the same unimpaired to succeeding generations, do ordain," &c.

Art. I. sect. 3. "Whereas, Almighty God hath created the mind free, and all attempts to influence by temporal punishment or burthens, or by civil incapacitation, tend to beget habits of hypocrisy and meanness; and whereas, a principal object of our venerated ancestors in their migration to this country and their settlement of this State, was, as they expressed it, to hold forth a lively experiment, that a flourishing civil State may stand and be best maintained with full liberty in religious concernments; we therefore," &c. Then follows a clause similar to that of Maine.

Connecticut.

The Preamble to the Constitution begins with, "acknowledging with gratitude the good Providence of God in having permitted them" (the people) "to enjoy a free government," &c.

Art. I. sect. 3. "The exercise and enjoyment of religious profession and worship, without discrimination, shall forever be free to all persons in this State: provided, that the right hereby declared and established shall not be so construed as to excuse acts of licentiousness or to justify practices inconsistent with the peace and safety of the State."

Sect. 4. "No preference shall be given by law to any Christian sect, or mode of worship."

NEW YORK.

Preamble. "We, the people of the State of New York, grateful to Almighty God for our freedom," &c.

Art. I. sect. 3. "The free exercise and enjoyment of religious profession and worship, without discrimination or preference, shall forever be allowed in this State to all mankind; and no person shall be rendered incompetent to be a witness on account of his opinions in matters of religious belief: but the liberty of conscience, hereby secured, shall not be so construed as to excuse acts of licentiousness or justify practices inconsistent with the peace or safety of this State."

NEW JERSEY.

The Preamble of the Constitution is identical with that of Rhode Island, given above.

Art. I. sect. 3. "No person shall be deprived of the inestimable privilege of worshipping Almighty God in a manner agreeable to the dictates of his own conscience." Then follows the provision, that no person shall be compelled to attend upon any worship or pay any tithes or taxes for support of any church or ministry. "There shall be no establishment of one religious sect in preference to another: no religious test shall be required as a qualification for any office or public trust, and no person shall be denied the exercise of any civil right, merely on account of his religious principles."

PENNSYLVANIA.

Art. IX. sect. 3. "That all men have a natural and indefeasible right to worship Almighty God according to the dictates of their own consciences; that no man can of right, be compelled to attend, erect or support any place of worship, or to maintain any ministry against his own consent; that no human authority can, in any case whatever, control or interfere with the rights of conscience; and that no preference shall ever be given by law to any religious establishment or modes of worship."

Sect 4. "That no person acknowledging the Being of a God and a future state of rewards and punishments, shall, on account of his religious sentiments, be disqualified to hold any office or place of trust or profit under this Commonwealth."

DELAWARE.

The Constitution begins, "Through Divine goodness all men have, by nature, the rights of worshipping and serving their Creator according to the dictates of their consciences," &c. "Although it is the duty of all men frequently to assemble together for the public worship of the Author of the Universe; and piety and morality, on which the prosperity of communities depends, are thereby promoted, yet no man can or ought to be compelled to attend any religious worship, or to contribute to the erection or support of any place of worship, or to the maintenance of any ministry, against his own free will and consent; and no power shall or ought to be vested in or assumed by any magistrate, that shall in any case interfere with or in any manner control, the rights of conscience in the free exercise of religious worship: nor shall a preference be given by law to any religious societies, denomination or modes of worship. No religious test shall be required as a qualification to any office or trust under this State."

Maryland.

The thirty-third section of the Declaration of Rights, prefixed to the Constitution, reads: "That as it is the duty of every man to worship God in such manner as he thinks most acceptable to Him, all persons are equally entitled to protection in their religious liberty: wherefore, no person ought, by any law, to be molested in his person or estate on account of his religious persuasion or profession, or for his religious practice: unless, under color of religion, any man shall disturb the good order, peace or safety of the State, or shall infringe the laws of morality, or injure others in their natural, civil or religious rights; nor ought any person to be compelled to frequent or maintain, or contribute, unless on contract, to maintain any place of worship or any ministry; nor shall any person be deemed incompetent as a witness or juror who believes in the existence of a God, and that under His dispensation such person will be held morally accountable for his acts and be rewarded or punished therefor, either in this world or the world to come." "That no other test or qualification ought to be required on admission to any office of trust or profit, than such oath of office as may be prescribed, &c., and a declaration of belief in the Christian religion; and if the party shall profess to be a Jew, the declaration shall be of his belief in a future state of rewards and punishments."

Virginia.

The sixteenth section of the Bill of Rights, prefixed to the Constitution of Virginia, reads: "That religion or the duty which we owe to our Creator, and the manner of discharging it, can be directed only by reason and conviction, and not by force and violence; and therefore, all men are equally entitled to the free exercise of religion, according to the dictates of conscience; and that it is the mutual duty of all to practise Christian forbearance, love and charity, towards each other."

North Carolina.

Art. IV. sect. 2. "No person who shall deny the being of a God, or the truth of the Christian religion, or the Divine authority of the Old and New Testament, or who shall hold religious principles incompatible with the freedom or safety of the State, shall be capable of holding any office or place of trust or profit in the civil department within this State."

South Carolina.

Art. VIII. sect. 1. "The free exercise and enjoyment of religious profession and worship, without discrimination or preference, shall forever hereafter be allowed, within this State, to all mankind; provided, that the liberty of conscience thereby declared, shall not be so construed as to excuse acts of licentiousness, or justify practices inconsistent with the peace and safety of this State."

In the twenty-third section of the first article, "Ministers of the Gospel" are rendered ineligible to the office of Governor or Lieutenant-Governor, or to a seat in the Senate or House of Representatives, on the ground that they are, "by their profession, dedicated to the service of God and the care of souls, and ought not to be diverted from the great duty of their functions."

Georgia.

Art. IV. sect. 10. "No person within this State shall, upon any pretence, be deprived of the inestimable privilege of worshipping God in a manner agreeable to his own conscience, nor be compelled to attend any place of worship contrary to his own faith and judgment; nor shall he ever be obliged to pay tithes, taxes, or any other rate, for the building or repairing any place of worship, or for the maintenance of any Minister, contrary to what he believes to be right, or hath voluntarily engaged to do. No one religious society shall ever be established in this State in preference to any other, nor shall any person be denied the enjoyment of any civil right, merely on account of his religious principles."

Florida.

Section 3d of the Declaration of Rights, prefixed to the Constitution, is, "That all men have a natural and inalienable right to worship Almighty God according to the dictates of their own conscience; and that no preference shall ever be given by law to any religious establishment, or mode of worship, in this State."

Alabama.

Art. I. sect. 3. of the Declaration of Rights, prefixed to the Constitution, is, "No person within this State shall, upon any pretence, be deprived of the inestimable privilege of worshipping God in the manner most agreeable to his own conscience, nor be compelled to attend any place of worship; nor shall any one ever be obliged to pay any tithes, taxes, or other rate, for the building or repairing any place of worship, or for the maintenance of any Minister or ministry."

Sect. 4. "No human authority ought, in any case whatever, to control or interfere with the right of conscience."

Sect. 5. "No person shall be hurt, molested, or restrained in his religious professions, sentiments, or persuasions, provided he does not disturb others in their religious worship."

Sect. 6. "The civil rights, privileges, or capacities, of any citizen shall in no way be diminished or enlarged on account of his religious principles."

Sect. 7. "There shall be no establishment of religion by law; no preference shall ever be given by law to any religious sect, society, denomination, or mode of worship; and no religious test shall ever be required as a qualification to any office or public trust under this State."

MISSISSIPPI.

Art. I. sect. 3, 4, 5. "The exercise and enjoyment of religious profession and worship, without discrimination, shall forever be free to all persons in this State; provided, that the right hereby declared and established shall not be so construed as to excuse acts of licentiousness, or justify practices inconsistent with the peace and safety of the State."

Sect. 4. "No preference shall ever be given by law to any religious sect or mode of worship."

Sect. 5. "That no person shall be molested for his opinions on any subject whatever, nor suffer any civil or political incapacity, or acquire any civil or political advantages, in consequence of such opinions, except in cases provided in this Constitution." (The exception relates to a provision against duelling. See Art. VII. sect. 1, 2.)

Art. VII. sect. 14. "Religion, morality and knowledge being necessary to good government, the preservation of liberty, and the happiness of mankind, schools, and the means of education, shall forever be encouraged in this State."

TENNESSEE.

Section 3, article I., is nearly identical with section 3, of article IX., of that of Pennsylvania, which is cited above. Section 4 reads, "That no religious test shall ever be required as a qualification to any office or public trust under this state." Section 3, of article VIII., empowers the Legislature to pass laws exempting from attendance upon private and general musters citizens belonging to any denomination known to be opposed to bearing arms. Section 1, of article IX., excludes Ministers of the gospel from a seat in the Legislature in nearly the same terms as are employed in the Constitution of South Carolina. Section 2, of article IX., reads, "No person who denies the being of a God, or a future state of rewards or punishments, shall hold any office in the civil department of this State."

KENTUCKY.

Section 5, of article XIII., of the Constitution, is identical with the 3d section of the 9th article of that of Pennsylvania, cited above. The 6th section is, "That the civil rights, privileges, or capacities of any citizen shall in no wise be diminished or enlarged on account of his religion."

Ohio.

The Constitution begins, "We, the people of the State of Ohio, grateful to Almighty God for our freedom, to secure its blessings, and promote our common welfare, do establish this Constitution." The seventh section of the first article is, in its first portion, nearly identical with the third section of the ninth article of that of Pennsylvania. The remainder is thus: "No religious test shall be required as a qualification for office, nor shall any person be incompetent to be a witness on account of his religious belief; but nothing herein shall be construed to dispense with oaths and affirmations. Religion, morality, and knowledge, however, being essential to good government, it shall be the duty of the General Assembly to pass suitable laws to protect every religious denomination in the peaceable enjoyment of its own mode of public worship, and to encourage schools and the means of instruction."

Indiana.

The preamble has these words: "We, the people of the State of Indiana, grateful to Almighty God for the free exercise of the right to choose our own form of government, do ordain this Constitution."

Art. I. sect. 1. "We declare that all men are created equal; that they are endowed by their Creator with certain inalienable rights," &c.

Sect. 2. "All men shall be secured in the natural right to worship Almighty God according to the dictates of their own consciences."

Sect. 3. "No law shall, in any case whatever, control the free exercise and enjoyment of religious opinion, or interfere with the rights of conscience."

Sect. 4. "No preference shall be given by law to any creed, religious society or mode of worship; and no man shall be compelled to attend, erect or support any place of worship, or to maintain any ministry, against his consent."

Sect. 5. "No religious test shall be required as a qualification for any office of trust or profit."

Sect. 6. "No money shall be drawn from the treasury for any religious or theological institution."

Sect. 7. "No person shall be rendered incompetent as a witness, in consequence of his opinions on matters of religion."

Illinois.

The Preamble contains the same words we have already cited from the Preamble to that of Rhode Island. The third section of the thirteenth article contains the same provision as that in the third section of the ninth article of that of Pennsylvania. The fourth section is, "That no religious test shall ever be required as a qualification to any office of public trust under this State."

Michigan.

The twenty-fourth section of the fourth article of the Constitution, reads, "The Legislature may authorize the employment of a Chaplain for the State Prison; but no money shall be appropriated for the payment of any religious services in either House of the Legislature."

Art. IV. sect. 39. "The Legislature shall pass no law to prevent any person from worshiping Almighty

God according to the dictates of his conscience, or to compel any person to attend, erect or support any place of religious worship, or to pay tithes, taxes or other rates, for the support of any minister of the gospel or teacher of religion."

Sect. 40. "No money shall be appropriated or drawn from the treasury for the benefit of any religious sect or society, theological or religious seminary, nor shall property belonging to the State be appropriated for any such purposes."

Sect. 41. "The Legislature shall not diminish or enlarge the civil or political rights, privileges and capacities of any person, on account of his opinion or belief concerning matters of religion."

Missouri.

The fourth section of the eleventh article of the Constitution, is the same in substance, and nearly in words, as the third section of the ninth article of that of Pennsylvania.

The 5th section provides, "That no person, on account of his religious opinions, can be rendered ineligible to any office of trust or profit under this State: that no preference can ever be given by law to any sect or mode of worship, and no religious corporation can ever be established in this State. No religious sect or society should be permitted to accumulate or hold in mortmain, large bodies of land or other property, and all extensive ecclesiastical perpetuities are dangerous to liberty: *Provided*, that any religious society may hold, in any assumed name, so much land as may be necessary for a house and buildings for public worship — for a parsonage and for a

4

burying ground, and for no other purpose whatever; but no congregation shall own for such purposes more than one acre of land in a town, nor more than ten acres in the country."

Arkansas.

The third section of the second article of the Constitution is the same as the third section of the ninth article of that of Pennsylvania; and the fourth section of the second article of that of Arkansas is, in substance, the same as the forty-first section of the fourth article of that of Michigan, cited above.

Texas.

The Constitution begins thus: "We, the people of Texas, acknowledging with gratitude the grace and beneficence of God in permitting us to make a choice of our form of government, do," &c. &c.

The fourth section of article first of the Constitution of Texas, is the same with the third section of the ninth article of that of Pennsylvania, the following sentence being added: "But it shall be the duty of the Legislature to pass such laws as shall be necessary to protect every religious denomination in the peaceable enjoyment of their own mode of public worship." The previous section prohibits religious tests as a qualification for office.

Iowa.

The Constitution commences, "We, the people of Iowa, grateful to the Supreme Being for the blessings hitherto enjoyed, and feeling our dependence on Him for a continuation of these blessings, do ordain," &c.

Art. II. sect. 3. "The General Assembly shall make no law respecting an establishment of religion, or prohibiting the free exercise thereof, nor shall any person be compelled to attend any place of worship, pay tithes, taxes, or other rates, for building or repairing places of worship, or for the maintenance of any minister or ministry."

Sect. 4. "No religious test shall be required as a qualification for any office or public trust, and no person shall be deprived of any of his rights, privileges or capacities, or disqualified from the performance of any of his public or private duties, or rendered incompetent to give evidence in any court of law or equity, in consequence of his opinions on the subject of religion."

Wisconsin.

The Preamble begins, "We, the people of Wisconsin, grateful to Almighty God for our freedom," &c.

Art. I. sect. 18. "The right of every man to worship Almighty God according to the dictates of his own conscience shall never be infringed." This section proceeds nearly in the words of section third in the ninth article of that of Pennsylvania, and concludes in these words: "Nor shall any money be drawn from the treasury for the benefit of any religious societies, or religious or theological seminaries."

Section nineteen is in substance the same as section four of article second of that of Iowa, cited above.

California.

Art. I. sect. 4. "The free exercise and enjoyment of religious profession and worship, without discrimination or preference, shall forever be allowed in this State; and no person shall be rendered incompetent to be a witness on account of his opinions on matters of religious belief, but the liberty of conscience hereby secured shall not be so construed as to excuse acts of licentiousness or justify practices inconsistent with the peace or safety of this State."

SECTION VI.

Remarks on the Constitutional Provisions cited in the Preceding Section.

THESE Constitutions of the several States are compacts between the people of a State collectively and each individual of the State. The citizens of each State are a Christian people, but opposed to Church establishments in connection with the State, and opposed to all spiritual domination. Being chiefly Protestants and entertaining a great diversity of views on the subject of religion, as is inevitable where men think and interpret for themselves, they felt the necessity of mutual forbearance and toleration; they perceived that whilst Christianity was an indispensable element of our free institutions, it was needful that it also should be free and untrammeled. These Constitutions then, emanating from Christian people, guarantee to each individual now living or hereafter to live under them, that he shall enjoy the right of worshipping God according to the dictates of his conscience, without restraint or molestation; that he shall not be compelled to attend, build or repair any church, or for that end pay tax, tithe or rate; that his civil rights shall not be abridged on account of his religious opinions; that no religious test shall be interposed to disqualify him for office, and that he shall not be incompetent as a witness by reason of his religious opinions; but they provide that the privileges thus granted shall not be abused by any immoral or licentious act, or any attack upon Christianity or any disturbance of its worship, or any act against the peace or safety of the State. Under these constitutional guarantees which a Christian people provide for their own security and peace, they invite all who are inclined, to come, subject only to the disabilities in which they acquiesce themselves.

These Constitutions make religion free by making its professors, its profession, and its worship free. Christianity claims no special establishment and no special power, civil or spiritual, under these instruments. Its security is higher than the Constitution itself: it is in the hearts and minds of the people who framed the Constitution. With certain qualifications, but in a very important sense, it is an element of our common or unwritten law. This, as we shall presently see, has been solemnly decided by many of our highest courts and ablest jurists.

As a Christian people, we lay one hand upon the Bible and say, "This is the Testament from which we derive our religion:" and the other upon the Constitution, and say, "This is our Social Compact, by which we mutually guarantee religious liberty."

Each Constitution exists as the work of a Christian people: it neither alters, modifies, enlarges nor abridges Christianity. It provides against all spiritual domination and secures full personal religious liberty. The liberty of worship so fully accorded, is the liberty to worship God, the God of Christianity, and not any other being real or imaginary. Christianity is not displaced but expressly recognized, though not defined. Its exercise is left with the people, its liberty is secured by the Constitution.

If no such constitutional provisions had been made, our judicial tribunals must have developed the common law doctrine of Christianity to the same effect, for our civil liberty would necessarily demand religious liberty and obtain it, where the people were the fountains of power. Our written Constitutions, our unwritten common law, public sentiment and the deep convictions of the people, are in perfect accord, that Christianity is the religion of the country and that religious liberty is the law of the country. All connection between Church and State is cut off here forever, all sectarian preferences are precluded, all spiritual domination is absolutely forbidden, as alike contrary to the spirit of true religion and dangerous to free institutions.

The benefits of Christianity accrue to the people individually through their individual piety, and to the State only through the piety and morality of the whole people. The only power of a church here, is the action of the people upon the government within the limits prescribed by the Constitution. The only expression Christianity can make of her wishes, is through the people upon their Legislatures and their laws, and upon their governments. There is a wide field here for Christian influence and action, without trenching on Constitutional limits.

We have yet to notice, before proceeding with our

remarks, a few of the decisions of our Courts upon the subject of Christianity. They shed a flood of light upon this neglected subject.

SECTION VII.

Judicial Decisions touching Christianity.

In 1822, a man was indicted in Pennsylvania for blasphemy, under an act of Assembly dated in 1700. He was convicted, and the case was carried to the Supreme Court, in which it was contended that the act of 1700, punishing blasphemy, was repugnant to the Constitution of 1787–1790, and therefore virtually repealed; and, moreover, that it was repugnant to our republican institutions, and to the rights of conscience. The opinion was delivered by Judge Duncan, from whose decision we make the following extracts:

"We will first dispose of what is considered the grand objection—*the constitutionality of Christianity;* for, in effect, that is the question."

"Christianity—general Christianity—is, and always has been, a part of the common law of Pennsylvania; Christianity without the spiritual artillery of European countries; for this Christianity was one of the considerations of the Royal Charter, and the very basis laid by its great founder, William Penn. Not Christianity founded on any particular religious tenets; not Christianity with an established church, and tithes, and spiritual courts, but Christianity with liberty of conscience to all men. William Penn and

Lord Baltimore were the first Legislators who passed laws in favor of liberty of conscience; for before that period, liberty of conscience appeared in the laws of no people, in the axiom of no government, in the institutes of no society; and scarcely in the temper of any man. Even the reformers were as furious against contumacious errors as they were loud in asserting the liberty of conscience. And to the wilds of America, peopled by a stock cut off by persecution from a Christian society, does Christianity owe, here, freedom of religious opinion and religious worship."

Judge Duncan then examines the English decisions in reference to Christianity, and shows that a man is not punished in England for holding erroneous opinions, but for so uttering them as to insult or attack Christianity. He quotes the words of Lord Mansfield, in Evans *vs.* the Chamberlain of London:

"The true principles of natural religion are part of the common law; the essential principles of revealed religion are part of the common law; so that a person subverting, vilifying, or ridiculing them, may be prosecuted at common law; but temporal punishment ought not to be inflicted for mere opinions."

Judge Duncan proceeds to quote, at some length, from the great statute of toleration, passed in Pennsylvania in the days of William Penn, in which it is provided that men shall not be compelled to conform to any religious observances but their own; but which also expressly provides against the creeping in of any looseness, irreligion, and atheism, under the pretence of rights of conscience. "And thus it is irrefragably proved," he remarks, "that the laws and institutions of this State are built on the foundation of reverence for Christianity."

He cites Judge Swift, of Connecticut: — "To prohibit the open, public, and explicit denial of the popular religion of a country, is a necessary measure to preserve the tranquillity of a government. Of this no person in a Christian country can complain; for, admitting him to be an infidel, he must acknowledge that no benefit can be derived from the subversion of a religion which enforces the purest morality." He cites, also, a decision in the Supreme Court of New York, in which it "was solemnly determined that Christianity was a part of the law of the land, and that to revile the Holy Scriptures was an indictable offence."* An attempt to overrule the law of this case was made in a subsequent Convention in New York, for the formation of a new Constitution, but it was repelled by a vote of 74 to 41.

Judge Duncan proceeds to say: — "No society can tolerate a wilful and despiteful attempt to subvert its religion no more than it would to break down its laws — a general, malicious and deliberate attempt to overthrow Christianity — general Christianity. This is the line of indication, where crime commences, and the offence becomes the subject of penal visitation. These offences may be classed under the following heads: — 1. Denying the being and providence of God. 2. Contumelious reproaches of Jesus Christ; profane and malevolent scoffing at the Scriptures, or exposing any part of them to ridicule. 3. Certain immoralities, tending to subvert all religion and morality, which are the foundation of all governments.

* For this opinion of Chief Justice Kent, see *infra*.

Without these restraints, no free government could long exist."

"It is impossible to administer the laws without taking the religion which the defendant in error has scoffed at; that Scripture which he has reviled, as their basis. To lay this aside is, at least, to weaken the confidence in human veracity, so essential to the purposes of society, and without which no question of property could be decided, and no criminal brought to justice. An oath in the common form, on a discredited book, would be a most idle ceremony."

"No preference is given, by law, to any particular religious persuasion. Protection is given to all by our laws. It is only the malicious reviler of Christianity who is punished. By general Christianity is not intended the doctrine of worship of any particular sect."

"While our own free Constitution secures liberty of conscience and freedom of religious worship to all, it is not necessary to maintain that any man should have the right, publicly, to vilify the religion of his neighbors and of the country. These two privileges are directly opposed. It is open, public vilification of the religion of the country that is punished, not to force conscience by punishment, but to preserve the peace of the country by an outward respect to the religion of the country."

"This is the Christianity, which is the law of our land, and I do not think it will be an invasion of any man's right of private judgment, or of the most extended privileges of propagating his sentiments with regard to religion in the manner he thinks most conclusive. If from a regard to decency and the good order of society, profane swearing, breach of the Sabbath, and blasphemy, are punishable by civil magistrates, these are not punished as sins or offences against God, but as crimes injurious to and having a malignant influence on society; for it is certain, that by these practices, no one pretends to prove any supposed truths, detect any supposed error, or advance any sentiment whatever." (Updegraff *vs.* The Commonwealth, 11 Sergeant and Rawles' Reports, pp. 394–410.)

This point was commented upon freely in the great case in the Supreme Court of the United States, arising upon Stephen Girard's Will. (*Vidal et al. vs.* The City of Philadelphia. 2 Howard, 127.) It was admitted by Mr. Binney, against whom it was cited by Mr. Webster, to be the law, in these words: "Christianity is a part of the law of Pennsylvania, it is true: but what Christianity and to what intent? It is Christianity without *particular* tenets; Christianity with liberty of conscience to all, and to the intent that it shall not be vilified, profaned or exposed to ridicule. It is Christianity for the defence and protection of those who believe, not for the persecution of those who do not. This is the utmost reach of the Commonwealth *vs.* Updegraff, 11 Ser. and R. 400. (Argument of Defendant's Counsel, 103.)

Mr. Webster in connection with his reference to this leading case, has the following remarks. Referring to certain great features in the Constitution and laws of Pennsylvania, he says: "These great principles have always been recognized; and they are no more part and parcel of the public law of Pennsylvania, than is the Christian religion. We have in the Charter of Pennsylvania, as prepared by its great founder, William Penn, we have in his "great law," as it was called, that the preservation of Christianity is one of the great and leading ends of government. This is declared in the Charter of the State. Then the laws of Pennsylvania, the statutes against blasphemy, the violation of the Lord's day, and others to the same effect, proceed on this great broad principle, that the preservation of Christianity is one of the main ends of government. This is the general public policy of Pennsylvania. On this head we have the case of the Commonwealth *vs.* Updegraff, in which a decision, in accordance with this whole doctrine, was given by the Supreme Court of Pennsylvania. The solemn opinion pronounced by that tribunal, begins by a general declaration, that Christianity is and always has been part of the common law of Pennsylvania."

"There is nothing that we look for with more certainty than this general principle, that Christianity is part of the law of the land. This was the case among the Puritans of New England, the Episcopalians of the Southern States, the Pennsylvania Quakers, the Baptists, the mass of the followers of Whitfield and Wesley and the Presbyterians, all brought and all adopted this great truth, and all have sustained it. And where there is any religious sentiment among men at all, this sentiment incorporates itself with the law. *Every thing declares it.*

"The generations that are gone before speak to it and pronounce it from the tomb. We feel it. All, all proclaim that Christianity, general, tolerant Christianity, Christianity independent of sects and parties, that Christianity to which the sword and fagot are unknown, general tolerant Christianity, is the law of the land." (Webster's Works, Vol. VI. pp. 175–176.)

Justice Story, in the course of the opinion delivered on behalf of the Supreme Court in this case upon Girard's Will, remarks: "It is also said, and said truly, that the Christian religion is a part of the common law of Pennsylvania; but this proposition is to be received with its appropriate qualifications and in connection with the provisions of the Constitution of that State."

"So that we are compelled to admit, that although Christianity be a part of the common law of the State, yet it is so in this qualified sense, that its *divine origin and truth are admitted,* and therefore it is not to be maliciously and openly reviled and blasphemed against, to the annoyance of believers or the injury of the public. Such was the doctrine of the Supreme Court of Pennsylvania in the Commonwealth *vs.* Updegraff." (2 Howard, 127.)

A man was indicted in Washington County, New York, in 1810, for blasphemy against the name of Christ. The offence was charged as against the common law, which is derived from England. The prisoner was found guilty, and sentenced to pay a fine of five hundred dollars and to be imprisoned for three months. The case was removed to the Supreme Court, the opinion of which was delivered by Chief Justice Kent, among the first, if not the very first jurist, which this country has produced. Judge Kent, after having noticed that the jury had decided the evil intent with which the words were spoken, proceeds to state the law on this subject in England, and quotes the Court of King's Bench, as saying in one case, "that Christianity was parcel of the law, and to cast contumelious reproaches upon it tended to weaken the foundation of moral obligation and the efficacy of oaths." And in another case, as saying, "they would not suffer it to be debated whether defaming Christianity in general was not an offence at common law, for whatever strikes at the root of Christianity, tends manifestly to the dissolution of civil government. But the Court were careful to say, they did not include disputes among learned men upon particular controverted points."

"Such offences have always been considered independent of any religious establishment or the rights of the Church. They are treated as affecting the essential interests of civil society."

Chief Justice Kent then proceeds to remark:— "And why should not the language contained in this indictment be still an offence with us? There is nothing in our manners or institutions which has prevented the application or the necessity of this part of the common law. We stand equally in need now, as formerly, of all that moral discipline and those principles of virtue which help to bind society together. The people of this State, in common with the people of this country, profess the general doctrines of Christianity as the rule of their faith and practice, and to scandalize the Author of these doctrines, is not only in a religious point of view, extremely impious, but even in respect to the obligations due to society, is a gross violation of decency and good order. Nothing could be more offensive to the virtuous part of the community, or more injurious to the tender morals of the young, than to declare such profanity lawful. It would go to confound all distinction between things sacred and profane."

"No government among any of the polished nations of antiquity, and none of the institutions of modern Europe (a single monitory case excepted), ever hazarded such a bold experiment upon the solidity of public morals, as to permit with impunity and under the sanction of their tribunals, the general religion of the community to be openly insulted and defamed. The very idea of jurisprudence with the ancient law-givers and philosophers, embraced the religion of the country. *Jurisprudentia est divinarum atque humanarum rerum notitia.* (Dig. b. 1. 10. 2. *Cic.* de legibus. b. 2. *passim.*)"

"The free, equal and undisturbed enjoyment of religious opinion, whatever it may be, and free and decent discussions on any religious subject, is granted and secured; but to revile, with malicious and blasphemous contempt, the religion professed by almost the whole community, is an abuse of that right. Nor are we bound by any expressions in the Constitution, as some have strangely supposed, either not to punish at all, or to punish indiscriminately, the like attacks upon the religion of Mahomet or of the *Grand Lama;* and for this plain reason, that we are a Christian people, and the morality of the country is drawn from Christianity, and not from the doctrines or worship of those impostors."

"Though the Constitution has discarded religious establishments, it does not forbid judicial cognizance of those offences against religion and morality which have no reference to any such establishment, or to any particular form of government, but are punishable because they strike at the root of moral obligations, and weaken the security of the social ties. The object of the thirty-eighth article of the Constitution was to 'guard against spiritual oppression and intolerance,' by declaring that 'the free exercise and enjoyment of religious profession and worship, without discrimination or preference, should forever thereafter be allowed within this State to all mankind.' This declaration (noble and magnanimous as it is when fully understood) never meant to withdraw religion in general, and with it the best sanctions of moral and social obligation, from all consideration and notice of the law. It will be fully satisfied by a free and universal toleration, without any of the tests, disabilities, or discriminations, incident to a religious establishment. To construe it as breaking down the common law barrier against licentious, wanton, and impious attacks upon Christianity itself, would be an enormous perversion of its meaning."

"The Legislative exposition of the Constitution is conformable to this view of it. Christianity in its enlarged sense, as a religion revealed and taught in the Bible, is not unknown to our law. The statute for preventing immorality consecrates the first day of the week as holy time, and considers the violation of it immoral. This was only the continuation, in substance, of a law of the Colony, which declared that the profanation of the Lord's Day was 'the great scandal of the Christian faith.' The act concerning oaths recognizes the common law mode of administering an oath, 'by laying the hand on and kissing the Gospels.' Surely, then, we are bound to conclude that wicked and malicious words, writings, and actions, which go to vilify those Gospels, continue, as at common law, to be an offence against the public peace and safety. They are inconsistent with the reverence due to the administration of an oath; and, among their other evil consequences, they tend to lessen, in the public mind, its religious sanction."* (The People *vs.* Ruggles, 8 Johnson's Reports, 290.)

A tradesman was prosecuted in Charleston, South Carolina, for selling goods on the Lord's day. In deciding against him, Judge O'Neal held the following language: —

"Crimes are classed into *mala in se* and *mala prohibita*. What gives them that character? We cannot answer as the Israelites would do, by pointing to Mount Sinai, and say the Lord God commanded us, saying, 'Thou shalt not kill,' 'thou shalt not steal.' The authority of these precepts comes to us through Christianity. . . . And hence the law delivered at Mount Sinai may be, by us, appealed to as pointing out that which is '*evil in itself.*'

"Again, our law declares all contracts *contra bonos mores* as illegal and void. What constitutes the standard of good morals? Is it not Christianity? There certainly is none other. Say *that* cannot be appealed to, and I do not know what would be good morals. The day of moral virtue in which we live would, in an instant, if that standard were abolished, lapse into the dark and murky night of Pagan immorality. In this State, the marriage tie is indissoluble.

* An attempt was made, in the Convention of 1822, to overrule the law in this case, but it failed by a vote of 74 to 41.

Whence do we take that maxim? It is from the teaching of the New Testament *alone*.

"In the courts over which we preside, we daily acknowledge Christianity as the most solemn part of our administration. A Christian witness, having no religious scruples against placing his hand upon the book, is sworn upon the Holy Evangelists, the books of the New Testament, which testify of our Saviour's birth, life, death, and resurrection. This is so common a matter, that it is little thought of as affording any evidence of the part which Christianity has in the common law.

"All blasphemous publications, carrying upon their face that irreverent rejection of God and His holy religion, which makes them dangerous to the community, have always been held to be indictable and punishable at common law. *Here* they would also be plain acts of licentiousness, having no warrant of protection whatever in our Constitution. This, however, never could extend to free and manly discussion on those holy subjects. For I agree with Mr. Jefferson (Notes on Virginia, p. 235): — 'Our rulers can have authority over such natural rights only as we have submitted to them. The rights of conscience we never submitted, we never could submit. We are answerable for them to our God!' But I should hesitate long in pushing the argument as far as he does, by saying that, in its exercise, 'It does me no injury for my neighbor to say there are twenty Gods, or no God.' While the argument rests only in words, it would be so evanescent that it might be no injury. But when it comes to be put in print, to be read like Paine's Age of Reason, by the young and unwary, where is the parent who would say, '*It does me no injury.*' I agree fully to what is said by Judge Duncan, in the Commonwealth *vs.* Updegraff (11 Ser. & R. 394), 'Christianity—general Christianity, is, and always has been, part of the common law; not Christianity founded on any particular religious tenets; not Christianity with an established church, and tithes, and spiritual courts; but Christianity with liberty of conscience to all men.'

"What I have said was not necessary for the decision of this case. It has only been said to prevent silence from being interpreted into a want of confidence in the proposition, that Christianity may be justly appealed to as a part of the common law." (From the Appendix to Matthews on the Bible and Civil Government, p. 248.)

SECTION VIII.

The social bearings of Christianity and the civil duties incumbent on Christians.

It is apparent, then, from our statutory and our common law, from our constitutions and our social institutions, that Christianity is legally recognized as the popular religion of this country. It is the very atmosphere in which our institutions exist; it is the cement by which they are bound together; it is the sanction of our penal laws; it is, in most cases, the security to which appeal is made by oath for official faithfulness; it is the guardian of judicial evidence; it is the basis of our morality, and the mould in which our civilization has been cast. The refuge we offer to men of all the world from intolerance, oppression and persecution, for opinion's sake, is offered under the influences of Christianity and according to its principles. We do not strike the Christian flag when we thus open wide our doors to the world, announcing that here is liberty of worship for all — Christian toleration for all: we rather invite men to come beneath its folds and under its protection. We spread over all that Christian vesture which is without seam or line of division, the broad mantle of Christian charity. We ask only obedience to such laws as are necessary to the preservation of such institutions — institutions which can only subsist and thrive under the Christian flag and on the broad ground of Christian charity.

Christianity asks no aid, and will receive none, from the State, to enforce its precepts or its worship. Its only power is moral, not physical. It seeks to govern men by the intrinsic excellence of its precepts, and by presenting to them the moral and religious claims of the Creator upon all His creatures. It seeks the extension of Christian civilization and the amelioration of human condition, the amendment of legislation and the wholesome reform of our social institutions, for the good of men as well as for the glory of God; but it expects to accomplish this good only by its moral and enlightening influence upon the minds and consciences of Christian men and those who lend themselves to Christian influences.

Christianity enjoys advantages here never before accorded to it by accident or by power. It wields no temporal power to make it feared; it wants no aid but that from its own friends. It enjoys for its generous toleration the heartfelt respect of all the intelligent and ardent friends of humanity. It only needs that the faults of its friends should be separated from the purity of its requirements; or that its friends should illustrate the purity of its doctrines by the purity of their lives, to give it a higher moral power and greater influence for good than in any position it has heretofore occupied.

The Christians of the United States have received from their Fathers the most important trust ever committed to men. The political institutions of this country, springing from Christian liberality, Christian civilization and intelligence, designed solely to promote human well-being, are placed in their hands as implements to be employed for human welfare. They contain powers safe only in the hands of those who are under Christian influences—powers fraught in their proper or improper exercise, with more of good or evil for the human family, than were ever before entrusted to Christian hands. The Evangelical Christians of the United States can sway this power at their pleasure, for they have heretofore been and still are, largely in the majority. There has undoubtedly been undue delicacy and forbearance shown in the exercise of this power. Such has been this forbearance, indeed, that the question now is rather of the neglect than of the abuse of power.

The principles of toleration and freedom of worship are so thoroughly interwoven into our State Constitutions, that Christian citizens who are the devoted friends of religious liberty, could not, without doing violence to their own feelings, infringe them; but a wide field for Christian enterprise and human advantage invited strongly their attention and their labors, without risk of transcending the limits of toleration or violating the rights of conscience.

Christianity is no mere negation in this country; it commands, or should command, the moral and political power of the Christians who dwell in it, exercised in accordance with the spirit of our institutions and with a view to the highest interests of men, temporal and eternal. The proper exercise of these functions of Christian freemen involves a wide scope of political and social knowledge. Have the Christians of the United States studied and comprehended as they ought, their position: and the problems which duty and opportunity have placed before them in that position?

The object to be accomplished by them was not the conversion of our tolerant into intolerant institutions; not to use their power to enforce Christian tenets; but to carry out, in a charitable spirit, that amelioration of the human condition which Christianity contemplates. Since the advent of our Saviour there has never been, on a national scale, so beautiful an exemplification of one of His two great fundamental precepts as that which is exhibited in the toleration of our Revolutionary Fathers, and in their offering to the poor outcasts of every clime a home so inviting, and institutions so liberal, as those of the United States. In fulfilling this duty, they but performed what Christianity made incumbent; they were the first body of Christian men to whom such an opportunity had been offered. They felt the obligation, and met it.

Can this be said of those Christian citizens to whom, in continuance, these important trusts were committed? What is the evidence that the Christian citizens of the United States have, since the era of our adoption of the Constitution, realized their responsibilities? Have they reflected that this national Constitution, and these constitutions of the States, are sacred trusts, for the due execution of which those who have the power and the intelligence to administer them aright are answerable? That they are talents committed to the servants of a Master who will require an account? "The powers that be are ordained of God," and obedience to such is the rule of the Gospel: in this country the responsibility of governing is added to that of obedience. It is a duty here to look to the powers which are to be executed, as well as to the powers who are to execute. The American Christian is entrusted with powers never before enjoyed by Christian citizens; — the power of naming those who are to be the "ordained of God." It has been the duty of Christians in times past, and is now in other countries, to suffer and obey; here it is our duty to designate those we are bound to obey. Obedience to the laws of the land, within right limits, is a Christian duty; but here Christians have the power of framing the laws to which they owe obedience.

It would be a mortifying task to inquire in what manner the Christians of the United States have fulfilled the unusual responsibilities thus placed upon them. The trust reposed in the people by the providence of God, was to administer the powers conferred by the Constitutions, State and National; the objects of the trust, and its limits, are indicated in these Constitutions; the majority of the trustees are Christians, or men professing to be swayed by Christian motives or preferences; — how have they discharged the duties of this trust? Taking into view the millions who inhabit this country, and their rapid increase; the multitudes who are hastening yearly to our shores; the power for good or evil of our institutions; the mighty influence of our example upon the rest of the world, it can hardly be conceived what higher duty any human being could have, excepting, only, the securing of his own salvation, than that which devolved, and still devolves upon Christians here to make American institutions as available as possible for human advantage. We do not allege that this duty has been wholly neglected; but how does the performance compare with the breadth of the obligation and with the facility of action? Christians here are sufficient in number to sway the whole policy of the country; but where do we mark their influence or their acts in the policy of the country? Have we not, alas! either to admit that Christians have failed to make their influence and their principles properly operative, or to confess that their influence and their principles are not Christian?

If we look into the party movements of the day, we encounter a scene of matchless wrangling, contention, and low intrigue, the object of which is, mainly, to get possession of the offices of the country and the salaries. There is scarcely an imaginable meanness to which party men do not descend — we may as well say there is scarcely a degree of moral degradation to which they do not descend—in pursuit of office. The manly independence which teaches men to seek a livelihood in some honest calling, is undermined, and large numbers of our people are trained to act as if no mode of living were so desirable as to be a feeder at the public crib, and nothing more praiseworthy than to be a constant beggar at the door of public patronage. The sentence which binds all men "to eat their bread in the sweat of their brows" is commuted, for them, into eating their bread by the sale of their honor, their honesty, or their independence. They abandon every thing honest in life to pursue every thing that is loathsome in party. How far Christian hands are soiled in such pursuits, let every one answer for himself. But it may be aptly inquired, could the machinery of party have fallen into such a shape, and could political degradation have descended so low, had the vigilance of the Christian citizens been in any degree proportioned to the interests involved?

If we look to the public elections of the country, shall we find in them, and in the events and processes connected with them, any marks of Christian influence or intervention? Our elections are, in too many instances, but the concentrated dregs of partizan intrigue and beggarly office-seeking. We know nothing more shameful, nothing more dangerous to our institutions, than the culpable neglect of duty on the part of good men, and the unrestrained sway of bad men, in the matter of our public elections. If Christian men have any share in this prostitution of public interests and private honesty, our elections reflect digrace not only upon the country, but upon Christianity.

Do we find any consolatory evidence of Christian influences in our Legislatures, State or National? Alas! they have become a bye-word of venality. We are far from saying there are no good men in these bodies; we do not even say that bad men could be kept out of them; but we do say that there are honest men enough—Christian men enough—to send a large majority of good, firm, and intelligent men into every Legislative Assembly in the nation; such men as would effectually resist the power of corruption, and consult only the highest interests of their constituents. That such men are not sent is fairly imputable to those who know it to be their duty, and having the power, yet wholly fail to fulfil their obligations.

If the legislation of this country in its two great aspects, State and National, be carefully regarded, it is chiefly difficult to say which is the most culpable, the defects of omission or those of commission. The guilt of omission appears to us far the greatest. Let us suppose that for the period of three score years and ten of our national existence, our Congress had been composed of such men as the people could have elected, what would have been the position of the country compared with what it is now, great and prosperous as is our actual position? So with the Legislatures of our original thirteen States and the eighteen which have been added. There has been, and is now, an attainable superiority to our past and present circumstances, which it is impossible to define, but which is appreciated by every honest and reflecting mind in the country. What has not been done for the population of this vast country, which might have been done, to promote the moral and material interests of the people, lies at the door of the Christians of this country, for they have most palpably neglected the political duties committed to them. The responsibility which rests upon a multitude, is, we know, seldom realized in its full force; but we fear the retribution which awaits the guilty, will be in some way individually realized, however large the multitude.

It is not safe then for Christians to infer, that Christianity and Politics have no mutual relations. Ours are Christian political institutions; they are not merely intended as convenient safe-guards, under which Christians may dwell in peace and quietness; they are not designed merely for the negative object of administering justice and protecting person and property: They are powers designed to be exercised for human advantage; they are facilities for complying with the great command, to love our neighbors as ourselves. We repeat it, they are talents committed to the hands of American Christians, the value and moment of which they have very imperfectly realized.*

* "Whence, save from the American *Church, can* go forth the light of a redeeming gospel to the dark places of the earth? If there be any philosophic reading of an historic Providence, then from *God's past and present dealings with us as a peculiar people,* and from *the evident signs of the times,* as displaying the powerlessness of all other nations for evangelizing a world; from these, I say, is the truth as apparent as an oracle of Revelation, that unto us, as stewards of the grace of God, is awarded the magnificent service of sending forth a full and free gospel over all the benighted continents of our globe—that from our beloved land, glorious in its scenery, and

That this responsibility is not realized by American Christians, is a fact they will not deny. The chief reason for this is not frequently assigned, but it should be not the less frequently sought; it is, perhaps, much more frequently felt than acknowledged.

---

its broad boundaries, and its new growth of civilization, and its loftier type of civil and religious manhood, the Angel that hath the everlasting gospel to preach, is already pluming the wing for flight over the nations; and that the hopes of the race, therefore, are not merely for *Time*, but for *Eternity!*"

"For we most frankly admit, that a religion that remains shut away from the common business of life, into the pure regions of spiritualism, as a thing of ecstacies, and sentiment, and psalm-singing: appearing statedly on Sabbath days, and in sanctuaries, and seen no more abroad during the six days of the secular and the social — We confess, I say, that such a religion, be it Christian or Pagan, is altogether out of place, and imbecile amid the restless and earnest tides of an age and a life like our own."

"But then quite as confident I am, that if Christianity have not hitherto acquitted herself to the full of all her secular and social duties; the secret lies not in her inadequacy to the work; but in the smallness of the sphere which Christians themselves have assigned her, and the class and kind of labor they have committed to her hands. Sure I am, at least, that as an intellectual and moral system, Christianity was designed for all nations and generations; and is divinely adapted to the exigencies of all nations and generations."

"Embodying, as Christianity does within itself, the mightiest and most practical moral influences to be found in God's universe; and revealed as the master contrivance of Infinite Wisdom, to restore man from his ruins, and bring back a wandering world to the light and the liberty of God's own children; it has only to be inaugurated in its place of rightful authority — only to be brought forth from the cloisters of contemplation, and the chairs of academic speculation — only to take hold in its strength, on the great practical questions of the race and the age, — and the scoffing world will acknowledge as they see, that an influence so long despised as a thing only busy with creeds, and ceremonies, and sacraments, can yet work gloriously and with a strong arm, as man's practical benefactor —

SECTION IX.

Denominational Differences.

THAT there should be differences of opinion in regard to many religious tenets, we regard as inevitable, where the mind is free to draw its own conclusions; and it is of the very essence of true Christianity that the mind should be thus free, that it may of its own motion, so far as human influences are concerned, and of its own comprehension, adopt the tenets which make up the sum of its religious belief. There is no excuse for men who profess to be followers of Christ, if, because they differ in some points of their religious belief, they should refuse to co-operate earnestly and efficiently together for the accomplishment of any

---

that its fostering is of every influence which makes up civilization—that its calling is unto the patronage of the arts, and sciences, and literature, and commerce, and trade—that its place is as truly in the cabinet as in the conventicle, in the senate-chamber, as at a sacrament—that it can acquit itself vigorously of all Social and Civil, in a word, of every secular duty; and is gloriously equal to all the exigencies of the times, and every possible emergency of the day and the generation."

"And we say, such an inauguration to a high sway over things merely temporal, Christianity deserves to-day, at the hands of its disciples. It deserves to be justified openly from the suspicions of the world, that it is after all, but a low, and paltry, and drivelling fanaticism. It deserves to be brought abroad from the closet and cloister, to enter as a living power into the philosophy, and speculation, and the earnest life, and all the high enterprise of an uprising Humanity."—*Rev. C. Wadsworth's Sermon on Religion and Politics*, pp. 21—26.

good result with which their religious differences have no connection. They are not less bound to notice the points in which they agree than those in which they differ. The good they can accomplish in concert should not remain unperformed because there may be differences of opinion upon matters which have nothing to do with the work which is to be done. It cannot be concealed that sectarianism has been the main barrier which has kept Christians from uniting their efforts for the common good, in the administration of public affairs.*

* We cannot deny ourselves or our readers, the pleasure of producing here the following passages, from the recent address of Dr. Duff, upon the occasion of his public reception in Concert Hall, Philadelphia, February 21, 1854 :—

" We have hitherto been accustomed, on both sides of the Atlantic, to look at each other's differences, rather than our agreements in the faith. It is in the very nature of division to scatter and sever, while it is in the very nature of coincidence to bind and cement. The former sows the seeds of discord, while the latter is the source of harmony. Why, then, should we not look rather at the points about which we are thoroughly agreed, and which are the great fundamental doctrines of Christianity — those grand transcendent verities which constitute the foundation of all felicity on earth, and the earnest of all real blessedness in heaven! And why should we not rejoice in the privilege of casting those comparatively minor points in the shade, in order that we may enjoy the full effulgence and beautitude of the latter?

"Let us cherish this '*unity of spirit*' more and more, and then we shall not be exhibited to the world as Christians throughout Christendom have been in times past, in an antagonism and turbulent collision, like the discrepant atoms of Miltonic chaos; but we shall be exhibited as bright celestial orbs, revolving in a grand and solemn procession of harmony and good-will, round the grand central sun, even Jesus Christ, the King of glory, and the King of saints. Doubtless, in the minds of many, minor differences will arise, for all

Sectarian differences have nothing in common with those which are political, and the men who differ

---

are not capacitated alike, or circumstanced alike, or educated alike; and wherever there is freedom of thought there must be freedom of speech; but if we cherish this *spirit of unity*, then will the strong learn to deal tenderly with the infirmities of the weak; and then will the weak be no longer disposed to quarrel with the (to them) unintelligible speculations or positions of the strong. Let us cherish this *spirit of unity* and brotherly love, and then, whatever differences may arise, we shall be all right in the main. From the very finitude of human nature there will be partialities, which will draw us nearer to one portion of the truth than to another; and from the very infirmity of our nature we are often led to dwell too exclusively upon one point, until it grows into disproportionate magnitude before our eyes, and we forget the points of higher importance — even as a pin-head, when brought into contact with the pupil of the eye, by gazing at it, it will render invisible the most beautiful landscape, or eclipse the very sun in the firmament of heaven.

"In this way too, we shall be enabled to remove a foul blot on Christianity. We shall dissipate the weakness of disunion, and, by gathering our scattered forces, we shall be enabled successfully to carry on the war of truth against error, into the very centre of the enemy's dominions. We shall be able to wipe away the bitter sarcasm that has been hurled by infidelity against the religion of Christ. Even while we all profess to be inhabiting a region so radiant with light and so exuberant with the bounties of a gracious God, that its marvellous history stands unparalleled in the archives of eternity, we all show our unbounded gratitude to the Author of such ineffable blessings, by cherishing an irreconcilable hatred to one another; while all are, by creation, the servants of one sovereign Lord; and may, by adoption, be called into his family to become princes of the blood-royal in heaven. In order to this, let us pray that our men of intellect may be men of seraphic fire — even the fire of Divine love, which alone can melt and fuse all into oneness of spirit; let us pray that all our sinfulness, all partiality, all envy, and all sinister motives, may be forever eradicated from amongst us, and that nothing may be allowed to interfere with the realizing of so glorious a consummation, short of the dereliction of some vital principle, or a base compromise of some divine prerogative."

widely upon religious questions might harmonize well upon the public interests of the country. It is seen every day that men of all denominations mingle, without difficulty, in public affairs. What we urge as the omission of Christians, is, that they should not, as a body, have studied the institutions and interests of the country, from the point of view which Christianity affords, and thus prepared themselves to carry the benign principles of their religion, so far as they were applicable, into public affairs, in the spirit of that Christian toleration which reigns throughout our whole political system. It is not intended that Christians should unite their influence or intelligence or their power, for any ecclesiastical advantage, or for the purpose of weakening the principle of toleration, but solely for the purpose of making our institutions as efficient as possible for good to our own population and to all men within the reach of their influence. It is not desirable that Christians should unite to exalt the power of the church or churches, or any mere religious power, but to do that good to men which Christianity dictates. It is, that Christians may not only show they are such, by doing good to their fellow-men as they have individual opportunity, but that they may vindicate their title to be the friends of Christ, by uniting to promote human welfare, through wise legislation, by discreet administration of the laws, and a just apportionment of national benefits.

Now, if never before, Christians should demonstrate, that the love they bear their fellow-men is as ready to act for their advantage through the medium of national powers as of private opportunities. If the

Legislative, Judicial and Executive powers vested in the public officers of our national government are capable of being so directed and administered as to confer extraordinary benefits, moral and material, upon the whole people, and through them upon others, it would be difficult to conjecture upon what grounds any excuse could be framed for those who have learned the bearing in these respects of Christian obligations, and who make no attempt to discharge them where the results would be so important.

It is an undeniable fact, that the Christians of the United States expend their chief efforts, we may well say nearly their whole efforts, for the welfare of men and the glory of their Master, in the direction of denominational advancement. That this effort has not gone unblessed, that it has borne abundant and rich fruits, we are happy to say. But, however blest these labors in their several narrow channels, they not only leave a wide scope of humanity uncared for and not reached, but they leave undone much that might be achieved by a union of Christians for great objects as to which they do not differ. These sectarian families may and should take care of themselves, but they should not forget that they too are members of a community larger than all of them united. As denominations, we cannot enforce our special tenets, our political institutions being constructed upon a more liberal principle; our duty as Christians is not limited by our power as denominations, but by the nature of the obligation itself and those whom it concerns.

We have many among us, very many, who keep out of the reach of denominational influence. Is there no larger platform on which these might be saved? Can no plan be devised for them? Is there no salvation out of the great denominations into which these can be inducted? We admit and admire what has been done by the Bible Society, the Tract Society, the American Board of Foreign Missions, and last, but chiefly, the American Sunday School Union. These efforts, however, instead of exhibiting what can be done by joint effort for the cause of Christ, only show what might be done. All these, and many more, might be sustained, without weakening denominational effort.*

---

* The following remarks are from the Sunday School Journal, of the 1st of March, 1854. They are sufficiently to the point to induce their insertion here.

"It has been said, not unfrequently, concerning efforts to propagate the Christian faith by a union of its professors, without respect to its denominational relations, that the truth must suffer severe wrong. In other words, that the various communities whhich are known by sectarian names owe it to themselves and to the cause of truth, to act separately in promoting the spread of religion, and by no means to consent to, or co-operate in, any scheme of Christian benevolence which constrains them to keep out of view their distinctive doctrines or usages. If they cannot be allowed to introduce those peculiarities of belief which distinguish them from the rest of the family of Christ, those who hold such opinions decline to countenance or further any plan of Christian effort which involves religious instruction.

"It is not our purpose, just now, to controvert this view. Its soundness is likely to be tested in good earnest, and it will not take many years to determine whether the sectarian phases of Christianity commend it most favorably to the consideration of those whom it is intended to bless and save. The experiment will be a costly one, however. If the perpetual or prominent exhibition of the controverted points of faith, and the discussion of them among those who hold in common what are known as the doctrines of the Evangelical church in its various branches, shall be the means of increasing the

The very spirit of our civil institutions seems to demand the construction, for a special purpose, of a wider platform. We offer a home to all, whatever their opinions; if they decline coming within the range of denominational effort, should not the Christians of the United States be able to offer them such religious instruction as, though it may not be Arminian, or Calvinistic, shall be strictly Evangelical? In a certain sense, as we have seen, Christianity is the law of the country; in that sense it is the very foundation on which our civil institutions are constructed, and, to that extent, instruction in it is not only essential, in reference to the eternal welfare of individuals, but to the permanence and continued im-

---

power of a corrupt but imposing hierarchy, or of multiplying recruits for the army of aliens and infidels, it will be no easy matter for the truth, as all our Evangelical churches hold it, to regain its present position, or to retain the means of diffusing itself which it now possesses.

"It is a question not unworthy of thought, whether the chief advantages supposed to be derived from sect-organization might not be retained consistently with a much more liberal course towards methods of propagating a common faith. Instead of an effort to make the peculiar doctrines or usages of a denomination of equal importance with the common faith, or even greater, let its advocates be satisfied with elevating them above the sect-doctrines or usages of other denominations, allowing to the common faith a superiority above them all. We are persuaded that if the voice of all who profess and call themselves Christians could be uttered this day, uninfluenced by party leaders and champions, it would be given, like the voice of many waters, for relaxing the cords which bind Christians in separate communities as sects, and for giving new strength and increased pressure to those which unite them as followers of Christ. THE SENTIMENT OF THE CHURCH, AT THIS MOMENT, IS FOR UNION — and the warfare of sects, like the warfare of states and nations, is waged by the will of the few at the cost of the many."

provement of our institutions. The indisposition to any such union of effort among those of differing religious persuasions, is a positive dereliction of Christian obligation. Whilst Christians keep faithfully with all the world their compact of religious toleration, not violating it in letter or in spirit, let them nevertheless pay all their Christian duty to the whole population abiding under that compact. The security for permanence to this toleration lies in the continuance of an enlarged comprehension of Christianity. Toleration so complete exists in no other country, and can only be sustained here by the moral force of these enlarged views. There is no denomination now in the United States which would, if completely in the ascendant, grant a toleration so large as that we now enjoy. This religious liberty, then, is a more enlarged conception than that of any one church. It is the spirit of Christianity which reigns over all of them which dictates it. Should not this spirit, this "general Christianity," as it is termed by Judge Duncan, be cherished, taught, and inculcated upon the people, and upon their children, as an essential feature of our civil polity, and necessary to its continuance? It is needful, even in the estimation of the unbeliever; for he has no security for his freedom of opinion and of speech, but in that generous toleration which springs from enlarged Christian views?

If souls are saved in the Methodist Church, in the Baptist, in the Episcopalian, in the Presbyterian Churches, are they saved in each Church by those doctrines which are regarded as peculiar to each? Or are they saved by that faith which is common to them all? If the latter, what must be said of those who are greater sticklers for the differences — the pe culiarities — than they are for the saving truths upon which all are agreed? If men will only take care of the great outer boundaries of their lands, they may remove their division fences without any injury to the fertility or productiveness of the soil; indeed, the land of any district might be worked with greater advantage without the usual lines of separation, if the owners could only agree. In matters of property this divisional selfishness may be excusable, but should the same spirit pervade the churches? Is the grace of God and the word of God to be hedged in by such lines? Should we be unwilling to save souls, unless they are first made Baptists or Presbyterians? After the great denominations have done all they can, in their separate churches, can they not unite to occupy that vast region which lies outside of all? If they refuse or neglect, on the ground of their differences, then they exalt their differences above that simple faith in Christ which enures to eternal life.

The Sunday School Union might, by a generous support from the principal Churches of the country, be placed in a position of vast power to do good. We have seen, however, within a few years, many proofs of a disposition to withhold from it all help and all countenance. The tendency recently has been visibly and unduly to separate action.

We are, however, not the advocate of any particular institution or any particular plan; our position is, that the Christianity which is common to the Evangelical denominations, is immeasurably more important than that which is in dispute between them. It is, therefore, the duty of Christians in the United States, to teach this common Christianity to the youth of the country and to all those whom the ordinary range of denominational effort cannot reach. And should not all Churches unite in this effort, by sustaining amply every institution and enterprise having this object in view? Christianity is of so liberal and expansive a nature, that judged by its true spirit, intense denominationalism, to which there is so strong an inclination and of which so many examples are multiplying before our eyes, is little less sinful than intense selfishness. They spring from a common source and may possibly incur a common condemnation. We doubt not, however, that the motive is often better than the deed.

If Christianity in a certain sense is the law of the land, and if in that sense it must be sustained and taught as a part of our civil polity, it becomes an imperative Christian, as well as civil duty, to define in what sense it is the law of the land and how it is to be inculcated. This duty cannot be ascertained nor fulfilled through any denominational agency. It is a duty which belongs to the community of Christian citizens and not to any family or denomination. No intelligent Christian need be asked whether our present civil polity would be safe if Christianity were banished from the land; and we may add, if human nature remains the same, it would scarcely be safer under the domination of any single sect. Power and wealth are too corrupting not to exhibit their effects rapidly in any community where they are exercised without sufficient restraint. The purity of our national character and of our profession of Christianity, is secured mainly under Providence by our manifold divisions — territorial, legislative, administrative, civil and religious. All these form so many mutual barriers and restraints, so many limitations of power, so many safe-guards of our liberties and of our national virtue.

SECTION X.

Special questions for the consideration of Christians in the United States.

THERE are great public duties then incumbent on the Christians of the United States and upon such citizens as acknowledge Christian obligations. They cannot, without a grave dereliction of Christian duty, confine all their love of country, all their zeal for humanity, all their efforts for the extension of the Redeemer's Kingdom, to the narrow sphere of denominational action; they must turn their eyes to the whole country and to its whole population, to ascertain what additional obligations lie upon them in reference to the entire social domain, in its civil as well as in its religious aspects. We have already intimated, that one duty of this kind met our fathers in their first steps under our present institutions — that of ascertaining and defining the legal and social position of Christianity. This subject has received so little attention, compared with its importance, that it may be regarded as yet to be performed. It is true, great light has occasionally been shed upon it and well defined opinions upon it have from time to time emanated from our judiciary, the purest of our civil institutions; but this light has not been concentrated, and these opinions have not yet been arranged and examined, with a view to determine their bearing and to ascertain how much of the field is explored, and how much and what portions remain to be surveyed. The work has been long delayed, and whilst the field has been unoccupied the unfriendly and the thoughtless have entered and sown broadcast the seeds of error. The delay has, however, furnished some valuable material and a large fund of observation and experience. If our fathers had, at the first, engaged earnestly in the adjustment of this question, they would have saved much mischief and forestalled many wrong conclusions, though they had lacked many materials for safe and wise determination. It has been regarded as a delicate subject; politicians were afraid of it, sectarians felt no concern in it, and the judges alone have brought to it any degree of courage and intelligence.

Without pretending to point out even the main duties which press most strongly on the Christian citizens of the United States, we indicate three as of urgent importance.

First: To discuss, define and settle the true position of Christianity in the United States, thereby showing what Christians may and should do here for the benefit of men, without departing from the principles of toleration which pervade all our institutions.

Second: To determine, prescribe and carry into operation that system of public education, including ample religious instruction, which is best fitted to prepare the rising generation for the discharge of all the social duties which are to devolve upon them, for the wisest and most efficient administration of our free institutions, for human advantage, and for that perpetuation and improvement of them which is so important to the future destinies of the human family.

Third: To consider, understand and establish the claims of labor. The masses of men here, as elsewhere, are laborers, working out the sentence which dooms man to eat his bread in the sweat of his brow. Vast multitudes are poor, and are often in danger of not finding the labor which will enable them to earn any bread. These men and their families, and their cause, should be one of the chief objects of consideration for the Christian citizens of the United States.

The first of these topics has been the chief subject of the foregoing pages: the last we reserve for a future paper. Our remaining remarks will be upon the subject of Public Education.

SECTION XI.

Public Education in the United States considered in its civil and religious aspects. Religious instruction in the Public Schools.

It would be strange indeed if special responsibilities were not entailed upon the Christian citizens of the United States on the subject of public education. Christian parents are always and every where under heavy obligations to train their children properly.

Not only the same obligations which press upon all Christian parents, rest upon them here, but many that are entirely new and peculiar to the position of Christianity in this country. There is, indeed, a training of the young in Christian families which is indispensable, as far as it can be secured, and is the same every where. Then there is that training for active and useful life which is equally indispensable, and not merely a private but a public consideration.

The nation which makes the welfare of its citizens a primary object, is just as much bound to care for the education of the young, as are the respective parents of the children. The duty of the parent stands first; if that is neglected, the State is *in loco parentis*. As one generation passes away, the whole concerns of a people are to be committed to the generation that follows. In proportion to the importance of the concerns to be thus committed to a coming generation should their preparation be, who are to assume these responsibilities. If our civil and social institutions have such a value as we have assumed them to have, and as they are expected to have; if our liberty, civil and religious, is worth preserving; if the highest hopes for human destiny are wrapped up in our republican governments; if Christianity itself is deeply interested in our national virtue and in our national prosperity, for the lessons we may give and the good we may do to the rest of the world, then surely the preparation of our children — all our children — the adequate public as well as private training which each succeeding generation should receive, should not fall short of what the whole power and wisdom of the State and the parents can bestow.

It is a preparation which cannot be left to the action of parents alone, not only because it would be unequally and inadequately accomplished, but because to a very large extent it would not be done at all. The State must at least furnish the means and facilities which a portion of the parents neglect to supply.

If education in a country should be at public expense as the most important concern of a state, it should be of universal application and as complete as possible in itself, because the public good dictates it, public safety requires it, and because the Christian principle is that we must love and care for others as well as for ourselves, and of course not deny to the children of others, the benefits we give our own, and least of all, deny to them the message of eternal life, and the benefits of Christian morality. To leave the children committed by their parents to the state, or those wholly neglected by their parents to the chance and motley education, especially in reference to their knowledge of Christianity, which they might or might not receive from their parents or under their direction, would be to abandon more than one-half the children of the nation to practical heathenism, to no education or a very imperfect one. The obligations of public and universal education are so generally admitted, that it is scarcely needful to press them.

In the present state of civilization and national intelligence, the question of national instruction for children cannot be left to the action of parents; it must be regarded at this day, and probably for a long time to come, as the most indispensable feature of wise national policy in a Christian country, to give all the children of the nation that training which will fit them for Christian citizenship.* The main problem

* The following decision of the Supreme Court of Pennsylvania, made at their December term, 1838, in the case of a Habeas Corpus to remove a child from the House of Refuge in Philadelphia, indicates very clearly the law of Pennsylvania, in the last resort on this subject of preventive education.

"To this end, may not the natural parents, when unequal to the task of education, or unworthy of it, be superseded by the *parens patriæ*, or common guardian of the community? It is to be remembered that the public has a paramount interest in the virtue and knowledge of its members, and that, of strict right, the business of education belongs to it. That parents are ordinarily intrusted with it, is because it can seldom be put into better hands: but where they are incompetent or corrupt, what is there to prevent the public from withdrawing their faculties, held, as they obviously are, at its suffering? The right of parental control is a natural but not an unalienable one. *It is not excepted by the Declaration of Rights out of the subjects of ordinary legislation; and it consequently remains subject to the ordinary legislative power, which, if wantonly or inconveniently used, would soon be constitutionally restricted, but the competency of which, as the government is constituted, cannot be doubted.* As to abridgment of indefeasible rights by confinement of the person, it is no more than what is borne, to a greater or less extent, in every school; and we know of no natural right to exemption from restraints which conduce to an infant's welfare. Nor is there a doubt of the propriety of their application in the particular instance. The infant has been snatched from a course which must have ended in confirmed depravity; and, not only is the restraint of her person lawful, but it would be an act of extreme cruelty to release her from it."

In a similar case, the Chief Justice of another state, holds this language:

"How deeply does it concern the community, to take these little creatures by the hand, when they shall have committed the first offence — withdraw them from contamination and guilt — provide the means of industry and education — soften their minds to the reception of moral and religious truth — and gradually, by gentle treat-is to determine what is to be the nature of this education, and how it is to be administered.

The highest wisdom of the country, the utmost Christian penetration is little enough to prescribe the course of instruction which should be given to our youth. They grow up together in the midst of the same social advantages and liberties, to administer and obey the same laws, to use aright or abuse the powers entrusted to them, to fulfil the social duties which Providence and their position has imposed upon them, or to fail at once in their duty to Heaven, to themselves, and to their fellow-men, disappointing the fondest hopes of the friends of humanity throughout the world. If we are right in our estimate of the responsible position of the citizens of the United States, we cannot be mistaken in taking a high standard for the education due to their children.

---

ment and wholesome discipline, lure them into the habits of order, truth, and honesty. Is there any greater duty in a Christian country than this? Is it not plucking brands from the burning, and saving souls from death? Is it not the cheapest and the best way of preserving the peace and tranquillity of the community, and guarding the fruits of industry?"

If the duty of the State to pluck these little brands from the burning be so strong and apparent, is it not equally its duty to search for the origin of the evil; and endeavor to sweeten the fountain of these bitter waters? Can it be, as some have asserted who ought to know better, that the duty of the State is simply the administration of justice,—to punish offenders but not to hinder the offence,—to stand immovable while the murder is in progress and then hang the murderer? Such doctrines flatly contravene the theory of our government, the spirit of our institutions, social and political, and the whole policy of our legislation. Government in the United States is no mere negation. It is still the depository of vast powers unexercised; it is for the people to call them into exercise whenever it can be done for public benefit.

Our fathers were trained in a severe school, in which with minds chastened by hardship they became rich in experience, both civil and religious. They have bequeathed to us our present position in the world and our social institutions, — the admiration of all people; their preparation for a task so successfully performed, was providential; our training or preparation for carrying on the great work of human amelioration which they began, should be specially designed and wisely adapted to the great objects in view. We can scarcely imagine any human position in which a whole generation of the young, upon whom the highest qualifications which a proper training can bestow had been conferred, could render such real service to the whole human family, as in the United States. There is here, then, every inducement which the world can afford, for conferring upon the young all the qualifications and fitness which education can give. The same reasons which evince its importance, prove that this education should be provided for all the children.

It is well known that the opinions of a large proportion of our intelligent people are in favor of a high grade of education; few schools have, in fact, yet reached the results which this large majority regard as desirable and attainable. It is very clear, indeed, that the desired result, for the entire population, can never be reached by any power, or any means, short of those only which can be employed by the State. The disjointed and unequal efforts, and the differing opinions of parents and Christian denominations, will ever stand in the way of any thorough and effective system of education independent of the State; the public at large, for there can be no other, is the proper umpire of these differences, the proper medium of concerted action, and the only adequate repository of power. There is no other resort in cases where the parents refuse or are unable to educate their children, or where they are disposed to educate them in a manner wholly inconsistent with our institutions.

There may be some disposed to question the Legislative power of our States to enforce the education of children. A little consideration will convince any one that there is no lack of power, when the people desire their representatives to employ it.* It may be a question of expediency whether a compulsory system should not be adopted, applicable to all who neglect to educate or to send their children to public schools. In one aspect, compulsory attendance upon schools may seem repugnant to our national prejudices. We know not whether any such system exists in the United States; that generally adopted leaves to parents the option of sending their children to the public schools, private schools of their own selection, or to no schools at all. It is evident that this is but the first step in a system of public instruction. It is perhaps safest, as well as most expedient, at present, in this country, to leave the parents to a choice between the public schools and those of their own selection. It cannot be admitted here as either sound or safe doctrine, that children may go wholly uneducated, if their parents neglect to avail themselves of the public schools. If the government of a

* As to the Legislative power over children, and the right of instruction, see note, ante, p. 92.

State has the power to prevent crime as well as punish it; if it has the power to check youthful delinquency as well as punish it, then the question being in what circumstances and at what age the neglected child shall come under supervision of public authority, it cannot be difficult to decide that the State may place the child at a public school before it becomes necessary to place it in a prison, house of refuge, or house of correction or detention. A shrewd Scotsman advises his countrymen rather to pay £30 to educate a child than £300 to try, imprison, punish, or transport a criminal offender.

Crime will ever be encountered, in every system of society, amongst the educated as well as the ignorant; but that a proper education is a preventive is as susceptible of proof as any other fact. It is well known, too, that it is far more economical to prevent crime than to punish it; but, if not more economical, what considerations, or what obstacles, should stand in the way of the preventive process, as a public measure, compared with the punishing process? On the one hand, we have all the advantage of making industrious and virtuous citizens, and on the other, all the disadvantages of having a horde of idle and criminal vagabonds, to grow up and crowd our prisons and penitentiaries for offences against life and property. No one can estimate the real evil to a country of such a population; and certainly no one should object to nipping such an evil in the bud, if needful, by a compulsory attendance upon the public schools. There should be no hesitation between a prison and a school; ignorance is crime enough to justify public intervention and an enforced education.

SECTION XII.

The kind of Education necessary, &c.—The Objections of the Hierarchy.

It may be said however, after all, that the soundness of these conclusions depends on the kind of education which is contemplated; and it may be inquired whether any adequate education can be imparted in a public school. These considerations are certainly met by the fact that, in very many respects, the best schools in the United States are public schools. This superiority extends to many departments of public education, and furnishes abundant reason to believe that these schools may, by proper effort of proper persons, be raised to a degree of perfection and efficiency scarcely conceived at the present time.

The objection that education in the public schools must always be defective because there can be in them no religious instruction is simply begging a great question. Our first reply to it is, that the Christian instruction imparted there must be exactly that which the Christian citizens of the United States determine it shall be; neither more nor less; for, within certain limits, they have power over the whole subject. As great misconception prevails on this subject, and as it requires, perhaps, some reflection to place it in its true light, we shall devote to it a few remarks, in the hope of provoking abler pens to the task of vindicating the Christian character of our public schools.

We deny emphatically that instruction in Christianity should be excluded from our public schools.

We aver with confidence, that there is a peculiar propriety and necessity that the schools of a Christian people should be Christian schools. We have shown by the highest authority, that Christianity is an element in the law of the country; that our civilization is Christian civilization; that the morality which is the basis of our legislation, and of our whole social system, is Christian morality; that the toleration which we have established among ourselves, and extend to all who come among us, is Christian toleration; that the oath or affirmation which is the security for all official faithfulness, from the highest office in the land to the lowest, and the guarantee of truthfulness for all judicial evidence, is an appeal to the Christian's God; that the days of fasting and prayer, and the days of thanksgiving, which are from time to time appointed by our rulers, are acts of national homage to the God of Christians; that the Chaplains appointed for our Legislative bodies and for the Army and Navy, and the compulsory attendance of soldiers and sailors upon public worship, required by law, are a national acknowledgment of God. With these facts in view, is it not a monstrous act of national impiety to deny all this knowledge to the children in the public schools, and all the reasons for this national homage to Christianity?

There has never been a more suicidal position taken by the most unwise of our politicians or statesmen, or the worst of our internal foes, than this exclusion of Christianity from public education. The worst enemy of humanity could not have devised a doctrine more dangerous to our republican institutions. It is fortunately too absurd, too monstrous, too unthankful, to take deep and lasting root in American soil. On a subject of such moment, frankness is, indeed, a positive Christian duty. It is not of American origin. It is the Papal doctrine of education for the United States; though not the Papal doctrine in Papal countries. Where Papal doctrine is complete or greatly preponderates, the education of the children is claimed by the Church as her prerogative, and she gives them a training strictly religious, according to the tenets of the Papal Church. In the United States this Church is the first and chief, if not the only objector, to religious instruction in our public schools.

This is the aspect of the subject which has perhaps most deterred inquirers from engaging in it. But the subject is of such importance, and freedom of speech is so indispensable to its proper treatment, that it argues want of manliness to yield a truth vital to our religious and political system, for want of courage to assert it. We are by no means insensible to the many faults of Protestantism, taken collectively; we have dwelt upon these faults with sorrow, if not with indignation; yet we feel bound to affirm, that the toleration of which we have spoken as so remarkable a characteristic of our civil institutions, is Protestant toleration, an emanation of Protestant Christianity. We cheerfully concede, that the Catholic laymen of this country are as truly patriotic and faithful to the country as other citizens; but the constitution of that Church did not grow up in our free atmosphere. It is the product of ecclesiastical and aristocratic power; it is still aristocratic in its government and irreconcilable with the theory of our civil polity in many important respects. The Church of Rome holds all without its pale to be heretics; and under its present constitution it neither can nor ever will, adopt or concede the principle of toleration; it may practise toleration from expediency, it may accept and use it as a boon or a stepping-stone to power; it cannot yield it as a principle.

Let it be mentioned to the honor of a noble Catholic, Lord Baltimore, that he was the first upon this continent to set the example of toleration; but he was not an Ecclesiastic, and did not, in so doing, represent the spirit or laws of his Church, or even secure its approbation.* There are thousands, nay millions, of intelligent Catholic laymen who would at this day, if free from Ecclesiastical influence, be as ready to promote toleration and freedom of religious worship as those of any Protestant denomination.

The position we take is, that the Papal Church is in its very essence, as its organs sometimes frankly avow, adverse to all religious toleration. In this respect it is, by its very constitution, adverse to our political institutions. The Christianity which, in a certain limited sense, is the law of the land, is Protestant Christianity: because, in its main feature, its chief characteristic, it is directly opposed to a leading doctrine of the Catholic Church.

Our State Constitutions are so many legal warrants for heresy; they expressly declare that men may worship God as they please, and guarantee to them this right. In doing this, no Protestant principle is violated, but one of the most binding laws of the Papal Church is flatly contravened. So strongly does this Church condemn heresy, that is, dissent from

* See Brownson's Review, October 1852, p. 453.

Papal practices and doctrines, that the oath prescribed to its Bishops on their ordination, contains a clause enjoining persecution: "*Hæreticos schismaticos et rebelles eidem Domino nostro vel successoribus prædictis pro posse persequar et impugnabo.*" *Heretics, schismatics, and rebels to our lord (the Pope) and his successors I will as far as I am able, persecute and attack.* There is, consequently, no country in which the Catholic Church is in full power, where men are permitted to worship God according to the dictates of their consciences; and few, if any, where they are not at this day persecuted and refused even the right of sepulture in a Catholic cemetery. We are sensible that there is much intolerance among Protestants, and there is no Protestant denomination which could be safely trusted with the power wielded in a manner so unchristian by the Papal Hierarchy.

It is a significant fact, that the only State in our Union which has neither granted nor guaranteed liberty of worship to all its citizens, is Louisiana. How far that remarkable omission is due to Papal influences in a State in which the Catholic Church is so influential, it should not be difficult to ascertain. It is desirable to know whether it be due to Hierarchical influence, to party truckling, or to recreant Protestantism.

The Papal Hierarchy then holds a principle, which when carried out, comes directly in conflict with one of the grandest features of our civil polity. It is necessary not to overlook this, because the Papacy goes steadily, by a determination which never varies, and a perseverance which never flags, to the establishment of her dominion over all other authority. In doing so, her Ecclesiastics are but pursuing the spirit and laws of her system; she claims to have an infallible Head, and may therefore very consistently claim precedence over all other authorities. Infallibility itself, as a claim upon the part of a church, is opposed to the spirit of our political system, which necessarily submits very many questions of Christian import, as that of toleration, for instance, to the decision of the people or their representatives. These two great features of the Papacy are inconsistent with our republicanism, and this truth should be looked in the face, not because that church menaces our national existence, but because the collision of these opposing principles must soon or late occur, and we should not only prepare for the contest, but we should, by way of prevention, let our position be understood.

There is, however, another reason for taking this view; it enables us to comprehend what is not generally understood, that the freedom of worship and the rights of conscience do not and cannot exist without limitation. The Papal claims of ascendency, persecution and infallibility, cannot be allowed under any claim of conscience or liberty of worship, for they are dangerous to the peace and safety of the state. The principle of limiting religious rights to those which are consistent with our national policy, is the more needful to be understood and insisted upon, because it may be necessary to apply it against religious usurpations by Protestants and others, as well as Romanists. It is necessary to the existence of our national and state governments, that they should be as fully endowed with the power of self-preservation on the side of religion, as upon any other side. Self-preservation is as much a law of national as of individual life; and danger to national existence may come in the shape of Ecclesiastical usurpation, Protestant as well as Papal.

When we speak of the Papal Church, we mean the Catholic Hierarchy, and not the *religion of the Catholic* people of the United States; for this Hierarchy claims power and maintains principles which have nothing in common with the religion of the laity. The property of the Church is held by this Hierarchy, and though many attempts have been made by the Catholic congregations of this country, to keep in their own hands and manage their own real estate, their claim has been steadfastly resisted and overruled; a virtual admission that their laymen cannot be relied upon for implicit obedience to the Hierarchy, or that the claims of the Hierarchy to absolute control are not to be modified, even in compliment to American institutions. Its selfish policy is unchanging; because it is the *fiat* of infallibility, it looks, as the proper result of its labors, to the conquest and absorption of all other authority, and to the conversion to that Church of all now devoted to other forms of Christianity, or to their extirpation as heretics, or to their complete subjugation as rebels against that Church.

The Christianity which is acknowledged by the United States as a nation, is that of the Old and New Testament, — the Bible. All denominations of Protestants receive this Bible as the rule of their faith; they do not coincide in all points in its interpretation, but by a generous concession among themselves, and by a generous offer to all who desire to live among them, they agree to establish a religious toleration so liberal and so ample, that men of every faith, and even no faith may live under it unmolested. This toleration, we repeat, so far from being an abandonment, is an exercise of one of the noblest traits of Christianity. Protestants, differing widely on many particulars, make this concession to religious differences, as they compromised also their political differences, and they offer the advantage of this wise concession to all the world beside. The Papal Hierarchy accepts this toleration, flourishes and grows under it, but it makes no concession, and yields not a particle of its enormous claims. It pushes forward with an unswerving pace to that full domination which, according to its principles, is its rightful destiny. It is contrary to its nature to make a compromise; it may submit to necessity or yield to a power it cannot conquer, but it steadfastly refuses any compromise, and will not abate one iota of its infallibility. It cannot, therefore, adopt the very first and most important principle of our institutions in the United States.

Offensive as are these principles, they are not too odious for our national toleration, so long as they are not manifested in overt acts, dangerous to the peace and safety of the state. We can look upon our Catholic fellow-citizens with the same friendly feeling that we look upon other denominations; *they* are Americanized, and partake of the spirit of our social system with its mutual concessions and compromises; we can extend to the Hierarchy, very few of whom are really citizens of the United States, and all of whom owe special and higher allegiance to the Pope, than they owe to this country, the same toleration we extend to others. Our national — our Christian duty, forbids the extension of that toleration one point beyond where the interests of the country and of Christianity require us to stop.

If we have succeeded in conveying to our readers, our own conviction of what is due to the present and coming generations of children in our republics, of the civil and religious obligations which will rest upon these children when they arrive at maturity, and of the facilities for doing good then to be enjoyed, they cannot fail to see that the church or denomination, which opposes religious instruction in the public schools, is at war with our institutions, with our civilization, and with the public peace and safety. That Bible, upon which the largest portion of the judicial oaths of the United States are administered, that Bible, which is the fountain of our Christianity, and which our whole system, civil and religious, assumes to be the Word of God, is the Bible which should be held up to the children in our public schools, announced to be a Revelation from the Most High, the will of God, the Old and New Testament of Christianity. It should be taught to the children to that extent, and in that way, which an enlightened and liberal piety would dictate.

The Bible is not a sectarian book in the eyes of Protestants, all their differences arise in its interpretation; it is not sectarian in the estimation of that Christianity which is an element of our national and social and legal systems. There must be a knowledge of the contents of the Bible which is not sectarian. Such is plainly the opinion of the Supreme Court of the United States in the case on Girard's Will, above referred to. Justice Story, admitting that sectarian religious instruction cannot be given in Girard College, proceeds thus: "Why may not the Bible, and especially the New Testament, without note or comment, be read and taught as a *divine revelation,* in the College — its general precepts *expounded,* its evidences *explained,* and its glorious principles of morality inculcated? What is there to prevent a work not sectarian upon the general evidences of Christianity, from being read and taught in the College by its lay-teachers?"

All Protestants unite in the circulation of the Bible without note or comment, because in their view, it contains the whole message of salvation to men, in the hope that the reading of God's word may alone lead men to consider what belongs to their eternal interests and to make their peace with Heaven. No denominational jealousy is exhibited among Protestants when men read the Bible without a clerical expositor at their side; neither can they feel any when it is read to, or by the children, in the public school; nor when its contents are explained without any view to those special theological distinctions which mark the lines of separation between Churches.

The Protestant denominations do not hold that there is no salvation except within the pale of some one of their various Churches; they do not deny that a man may attain, by the knowledge of the Bible alone, to the hope of a happy eternity, although he may know nothing of the lines of demarcation between the various Churches. Without undervaluing theology or denominational distinctions, which bespeak higher attainments in, or minuter knowledge of the Scriptures; there is then a knowledge, a saving knowledge, which may not partake of a sectarian character. It is in this very simple but comprehensive sense that Christianity is the religion of the country, that it is an element of our common law, that it speaks in the various Constitutions of the States, declaring religious liberty and securing freedom of worship and the rights of conscience. Whatever value denominations may attach to their exclusive tenets, and whatever force may be given to truth from their respective points of view, and whatever vigor of action may be attainable by such special associations of Christians holding the same doctrines, there is nevertheless what Judge Duncan calls a "general Christianity," derived from the Scriptures, under the light of which men may be saved. All truly good men of every Church, whilst they look upon their own system as the safest and best, yet rejoice as much over the sinner who repents with a knowledge of the Bible only, as if he repent with the aid of the catechism and the creed and clerical teaching. How unbecoming, how unchristian! to sneer, as some do, at any form of Christianity by which men may be saved; to scorn the only form of Christianity which the free circulation of the Bible can produce among those who have no access to denominational teaching.

We have been minute upon this point, to bring out more clearly the distinction between our Protestant, or American system of Christianity, and that avowed by the Papal Hierarchy. It is of vital consequence to our political system that this distinction be understood and its bearings comprehended. The Papal system denies that men can be saved out of the pale of that Church; it denies the principle of toleration; it acknowledges no other Church; it makes no concession nor compromise; it claims to have an infallible head, in the Pope, and not only refuses to accept the Bible as the chief expositor of Christianity, but objects to its circulation and perusal among its own people, and strenuously resists its introduction into the public schools. This issue between the country and the Papacy has long since been made up; it should long since have been decided. The hesitation and the ignorance displayed upon this question are equally disgraceful to us.

Our republican system demands intelligence, with moral and religious training, to fit citizens for the discharge of their responsible duties; it demands an open Bible, a "general Christianity," freedom of opinion and liberty of worship; it demands what the Papacy regards and denounces as heresies, and what its principles and laws require it to punish as such where it has the power, and what it does punish as such where it has the power. We cannot avoid, and should not postpone, the great questions now pending between our national system and the Papacy. The latter is a positive, active, pervading system; if we retreat, it pursues and occupies our position; if we neglect to go forward, it blocks our way. Ours may be a positive, pervading system, if we make it so. We have not the advantage of that singleness of purpose and special energy which belongs to the action of a single body or church; but we should have the advantage of larger and more liberal views, greater intelligence and greater moral power, from acting in harmony with our own institutions, if our various Churches were to unite their wisdom and energies for national purposes, as they might do, without any sacrifice of denominational usefulness or success.

Our American system requires the contents of the Bible to be taught in the public schools, for the reason that Christianity is an element of our political system, and the Bible is the source of Christianity. The Papal system rejects the Bible and its teachings from the public schools, because the Bible endangers their religious system. Shall we carry out our system, or yield and permit the Hierarchy to carry out theirs? Upon this subject the whole people of this country is arrayed against the Papal Church. If we yield this point, we surrender the principle of toleration and the right of private judgment, and virtually violate a provision contained in the Constitution of nearly every State in the Union — that there shall be no preference given to any church or denomination; for, by excluding the Bible from the school, at the instance of the Papacy, we give the Papal Church a direct preference, by adopting its system and rejecting our own.

If we construe the rights of conscience in that unlimited sense which some think the term implies, the Papal system will alone sever every bond of union— every obligation of our governments and Constitutions, civil and religious. Christianity, as incorporated into our American system, regards the Bible as the only revelation of God's will, and the only message of eternal life; our laws recognize no other Christianity than that of the Bible; the Papal Church professes to be of equal authority with the Bible, which it regards as only a portion of the direct teaching of God; the Papacy claims now, and at all times, to be the hand and the voice of God upon the earth. Our American system not only permits, but secures the right of all men to worship God as they severally prefer; and this is the American idea of the right of conscience. The Papacy pronounces this to be the right of heresy, as directly in opposition to their religious system, and to their rights of conscience. These contradictions cannot be reconciled. Our American system refers all questions of authority to the people, as the fountain of all our political power; the Papal system refers all questions of power ultimately to the Church, or its infallible head, by which it professes to decide upon the validity of every power, and upon the validity of every exercise of authority. According to the Papal interpretation of the right of conscience, it is the right to carry out their religious system in all its parts, one chief part of which is to recognize no other Church, and permit no other, for the very good reason, in their view, that no soul can be saved in any other. Christianity, as incorporated in our institutions, involves rights of conscience also, and these involve conscientious obligations to sustain and carry out the only system which gives and secures religious freedom.

The question then recurs, shall the advocates of religious freedom in the United States insist upon their rights of conscience, or shall they yield and allow the Papal right of conscience to prevail? We know that many entertain the view which it is one of our chief objects to controvert, that there is no particle of Christianity in our political system, and that, therefore, the right of conscience does not permit us to advance positive claims in behalf of

Christianity, but only requires us not to do any thing in the name of Christianity to which any one objects on the score of conscience. Our system is no such absurdity as to be reducible to zero by the conflicting pretensions of either Papal or infidel objectors; it is a grand, original, expansive, and positive system of Christian toleration, with civil and religious liberty. We are religiously bound to maintain it at every hazard. We cannot retreat and leave a territory occupied by neither party; we must not proclaim this nation to be Godless; we cannot say this is no longer a Christian nation; besides, whatever inch of ground we yield will be at once in Papal possession. Their *claim* already covers all: when we retreat, they are *in possession*. When their power is great enough to enforce their doctrines, toleration and religious liberty and rights of conscience are at an end. The Papacy tenders no consoling substitute; not even a modification, or amendment, or counterpart of our American system, civil or religious, but simply the Papal System, of which the world has had, and is now having, such experience as can leave us in no doubt of its qualities.

In one view there is no discrepancy between the Catholic religion and the Christianity of the United States. The laity of that church can enjoy their rights of conscience, and liberty of worship, in perfect harmony with other Christians. It is with the Ecclesiastical government of that Church that the difficulty began, and that government is wholly in the hands of Ecclesiastics; their people have no authority nor function in the government of their church. There is, then, no obstacle in the way of Catholic piety or

Catholic worship; it is the law of the Romish Ecclesiastical government which is at absolute war with our whole system, civil and religious. At present, our system is the strongest and ought to be carried faithfully into effect as the only means of preventing theirs from becoming the strongest, for when it does become the strongest, *it will be enforced.* Our delicacy forbids us to enforce our rights; their doctrine and duty commands them to enforce their system. But this is not the chief reason why ours should be carried into effect; if the Christian element be withdrawn, or, what is the same thing, if it is not taught, our social system has no bond; it becomes subject to the very reproaches which the Papacy fling at us, that we are verging to Paganism, that we have no unity, that we have no common faith. This will, indeed, be our case if we yield before the rights of conscience asserted by others without setting up and maintaining our own — if our devotion to religion is in going backward, and not in pressing forward; if we restrict ourselves to punishing men for blasphemy, for offences against good morals, for vilifying Christianity, and take no note of the spirit of a whole Priesthood which dooms every man professing this religion, which our law protects, to eternal damnation; which pronounces the Protestants of the United States, constituting nine-tenths of the inhabitants, heretics and schismatics, undeserving even of Christian burial. The law of Christian toleration requires us, and Christian charity requires us, to give these men a home among us; but they do not require us to shut our eyes to these facts; they do not require us to omit the vindication and teaching of that Christianity which is the basis of our whole civil and religious system. If we may punish a man for vilifying Christianity—our Christianity—should we not regard that as an offence in the Hierarchy, when they proclaim that ours is no Christianity at all, and that no soul can, by any possibility, be saved by it? Which should be the most offensive in our view, the miserable blasphemy, or the priestly denunciation?

We do not make such remarks to raise a clamor against the Romish Priesthood, or to call down upon them popular vengeance. Heaven forbid! Every attack upon the property and lives of Catholics disgraces and violates our system, and strengthens theirs. Let them have toleration and liberty of worship, with all the civil rights we have to give; that is our compact: but let us be true to ourselves and to the world—true to God; let us uphold and assert *that Christianity which teaches toleration, and secures liberty of worship.* And if we have in the midst of us a powerful and ambitious band of Ecclesiastics, who condemn the system which is our boast, and regard ours as no Christianity; who would put an end to religious freedom and the right of private judgment, let us meet this formidable enemy only by a more firm and constant vindication of that religious system which we regard as the safest for all men, as well Catholics as Protestants, and which, at any rate, is indispensable to the continuance of our national institutions.

Let not our friends become more dangerous than our enemies. Let us not betray Protestant Christianity, for upon it depends the validity of the principles of religious toleration, the rights of conscience, the right of private judgment, and liberty of worship. If we have no punishment for a system which denies all these principles — and we need none, for these principles imply none—let us at least more faithfully and vigorously propagate that new system of Christianity from which these principles spring, and overcome our enemy by heaping coals of fire upon his head.*

SECTION XIII.

The Policy of Public Schools adopted in the United States. — The necessity of Religious Instruction. — Denominational difficulties. — The Nature of the Religious Instruction to be given in them.

Public Schools are already the policy of the people of the United States. More than two-thirds of the States have already such schools in operation. Congress has provided an ample fund for their sustenance in all the States in which there is public land. American schools are spoken of throughout the world, where there is question of public education, as among the best in existence. The adoption of this system of public education by the governments of so many States, and the liberal provision made by Congress, indicate that the sentiments of the people in those States are favorable to the system. We run no risk in saying that the intelligent and evangelical portion of the people have brought about this decision. In point of fact, it is well known that these have been the active friends of the public school system. The

---

* See Appendix A.

people are committed to it; their chief duty, after adopting it, is to make it efficient, and to make it adequate. It is well known that these schools have been improving in every State, and that they are the subject of anxious attention and effort on the part of the various public authorities and Legislatures of the States in which they are in operation.

Whilst the sentiment of the country has been in favor of public schools offering the advantage of the same education to all, it has also frequently been clearly expressed in various ways, in favor of religious instruction in these schools; but this has not been carried out as generally and as firmly as its importance demanded. Another obstacle kept in the back-ground, has had its influence in retarding the adjustment of this subject of religious education in the public schools. A considerable number of good people, in every denomination of Christians, are afraid to countenance any religious instruction which is not denominational. They hold, that the distinctive features of their several churches, should be so early graven upon the tender minds of the children, as to be ever after ineffaceable. If their doctrines are sound, and they only adhere to them because they regard them as sound, they cannot be too early, nor too effectually, as they contend, impressed upon the minds of the children. They perceive the difficulty as among themselves, of carrying out such views in the public schools, and they stand aloof from the question of public religious instruction. They desire to see children religiously educated, and earnestly insist upon it, but between their devotion to the principle of Christian toleration, which they are afraid of violating, and their devotion to doctrinal distinctions, they stand paralyzed, and permit truth to be sacrificed, and the public interests to suffer, and children to go without religious instruction.

We think that all these difficulties, great as they appear, in a cause involving so many considerations vital to the welfare of our whole country, and indeed of the whole human family, can be surmounted, and should be surmounted. The spirit of concession, upon which our institutions are founded, is not yet exhausted; it is just as necessary in the progress of our history, as in its origin. When, as a people, we cease to act in the spirit of our institutions, they will come rapidly to an end. In one sense, it is true there can be no compromise in religious matters; that which is vital to Christianity cannot be surrendered, nor even kept out of view. The Bible cannot be sacrificed, nor kept out of view, to conciliate prejudices of any, whether priest or infidel. It is the manual of Christianity. We cannot concede that the Bible is a mere human production, because it is of the very essence of Christianity, that the Bible is a revelation from God. Christian toleration, however liberal it may be, assumes and reserves these truths; it is because the Bible teaches it, that toleration exists. He who commands us to love our neighbor as ourselves, countenances no intolerance, but releases us from no portion of our religious duty. When we come to the interpretation of the Bible, human fallibility intervenes, and differences arise. We would not undervalue doctrinal distinctions and denominational differences: they are inevitable, and inseparable from true religious liberty. They are, therefore, in the order of Providence, and it is easy to see, that many good results may flow from them, in giving variety and energy to Christian life, and in promoting a spirit of inquiry, with habits of deeper thinking and sharper discrimination.

But these higher ultimate attainments, though necessary to denominational strength and success, are not indispensable to salvation; sound theology is requisite to those who make any progress in theology: it is necessary for those, whose taste or position leads them to a prolonged study of the Bible, or to deep study in religious subjects.

How large a majority of our community, and of every other Christian community, stop short of any progress in theology, or any prolonged study of the Bible! Happily for such, though ignorance is no excuse in our land, the way to salvation is so simple, that he that runs may read, and "wayfaring men, though fools, shall not err therein." Upon how little theological knowledge, after all, throughout the membership of our most intelligent churches, is the faith and hope of many true Christians founded! Perhaps some of the purest and humblest Christians in the whole country, some, whose faith is the most immovably steadfast, are those who know scarce anything but Christ, and Him crucified. It was not among the wise and learned, that Christ found his first and most ardent disciples, and it is evident, that the comprehension of the Apostles themselves, up to the time of the resurrection of our Lord, was very limited as to many of the truths their Master had inculcated upon them. It is still true, that salvation is possible, and not unfrequent, without knowledge of theology as a science, and with a very limited knowledge of the contents of the Bible itself; it is still true and proper to say, "Believe on the Lord Jesus Christ, and thou shalt be saved, and thy house," and to this belief it is possible some might attain, whose whole religious instruction has been confined to the four Evangelists. We are not excusing ignorance, nor pleading for it, nor recommending it. We desire an admission of the fact, that remission of sins and the hope of a happy eternity, may be secured even by those whose attainments are thus limited. If this be so, there is a "general Christianity" in which men may be saved, who belong to no particular denomination, and are instructed in no peculiar tenets.

We are aware, that earnest and well-informed men of the various churches, regard this idea of general Christian knowledge, as compared with their special views, with a sort of contempt, if not of abhorrence, though they not unfrequently seem to hope, that individuals who have departed this life with no other knowledge, have secured their eternal peace. We think that this contempt or abhorrence, though natural to those whose whole life is spent in defending and teaching peculiar tenets, is highly censurable, if not very sinful. Whilst we may, and should do all we can to propagate our special tenets, if we believe them to be most sound, we should be none the less anxious that men should make their peace with God, even without embracing the minutiæ of our own creeds. Whilst we strengthen and defend our own more specific and narrow platform, and induce as many as we can to come upon it, we must neither frown upon, nor discourage those, who are standing upon a broader platform, whose lines are less specific, if upon that they can make their peace with Heaven. The simple fact that Protestants admit, that men may be saved in any Christian community in which the essential truths of Christianity are professed, proves that there is a common ground on which all might meet if they would. They may defend their peculiar views with all the pertinacity which they believe to be due to truth, but they should prize far the highest, those truths which are held in common by all true Christians, for such truths must, of necessity, be vital and important. How often, and alas! how much in vain are Christians exhorted to dwell more upon the points of their agreement, and less upon their differences! We suffer the strictness and exclusiveness of denominational teaching to harden our hearts,* and check that union and co-operation of different churches, upon which depends absolutely the success of many of our greatest Christian enterprises.

"I must say, that I consider it infinitely more characteristic of the religion we profess — the religion of peace and charity — that instead of each denomination sitting aloft and apart on its own hill, and frowning upon each other from their respective orbits, they should hold kindly and mutual converse, and see each other eye to eye, while they will discern to their mutual astonishment, if not how thoroughly, at least how substantially, they are at one. Now is the time to rally about the common standard of all that is pure and vital in Protestantism."† We regard the "common standard" here spoken of, as denoting the

* "Is Christ divided?" nothing else, is the reply we make.

† Dr. Chalmers's address to General Assembly of 1843.

same thing which Judge Duncan calls "general Christianity;" and the same which is intended by Chief Justice Kent, and the same which dictates toleration and liberty of worship, in our various State institutions. It has not been defined, vindicated and proclaimed, because Christians have spent their strength upon these differences, and not upon their agreement.

The question then returns, shall not the Christianity of the broader platform by which men may secure remission of sins and peace with God, this general Christianity which Judges Kent, Duncan and Story, pronounce to be part of the common law of the country, this "common standard" about which Dr. Chalmers called upon his countrymen to rally, this beneficent Christianity which speaks toleration in the constitutions of our States, and invites men of every creed and clime to our shores, our hospitality, and our protection, that Christianity which is the basis of our civilization, the fountain of our morality, the sanction of our official and judicial oaths, that religion which is preached by Chaplains to our various Legislative bodies, and to our Army and Navy, be taught in our schools, and be made known to our children? And if not, shall the reason be given that we insist more strenuously upon the points of difference, than upon the points of agreement; that we are more bent upon the teaching of our peculiarities, than upon the teaching of our essentials? Shall it be said, to the injury of Christianity, that we prefer to have children go without religious instruction, rather than have them instructed in the "common standard?" This spirit, which is a reproach to Christians, is fatally indulged at this moment throughout this country; let every man who entertains it, examine himself anew, to see whether he is not forgetting Him, who said, "Suffer little children to come unto me, and forbid them not." This voice should be heard in every school in the land, as it repeats, "Suffer little children to come unto me;" and no child should grow up without being taught from whom this invitation comes and how deeply he is interested in it.

SECTION XIV.

Professor Stowe's Report on Public Schools, made to the Governor of the State of Ohio. "Thoughts on Popular Education."

We gladly call to our aid a witness who has bestowed the most earnest and enlightened attention upon this subject. Professor C. E. Stowe was appointed by the Governor of the State of Ohio, in 1836, to visit the educational institutions of Europe, and make report of such matters as might appear to him worthy of their attention in Ohio. In speaking of the system of Prussia, which, in his opinion, combined more advantages than any other, he says, among other things, "In regard to the necessity of moral instruction, and the beneficial influence of the Bible in schools, I inquired of all classes of teachers and men, of every grade of religious faith, instructors in common schools, high schools and schools of art, of professors in colleges, universities and professional seminaries, in cities and in the country, in places where there was a uniformity, and in places where there was a diversity of creeds, of believers and unbelievers, of rationalists and enthusiasts, of Catholics and of Protestants; and I never found but one reply, and that was, that to leave the moral faculty uninstructed was to leave the most important power of the human mind undeveloped, and to strip education of almost every thing that can make it valuable; and that the Bible, independently of the interest attending it, as containing the most ancient and influential writings ever recorded by human hands, and comprising the religious system of almost the whole of the civilized world, is in itself the best book that can be put into the hands of children, to interest, to exercise, and to unfold their intellectual and moral powers. Every teacher whom I consulted, repelled with indignation, the idea that moral instruction is not proper for schools; and spurned with contempt the allegation, that the Bible cannot be introduced into common schools without encouraging a sectarian bias in the matter of teaching; an indignation and contempt which, I believe, will be participated in by every high-minded teacher in Christendom."

After describing with some particularity, the mode of religious instruction adopted, which embraced a pretty thorough knowledge of the great moral and religious truths of the Bible, its didactic lessons, and its important narratives; the Professor remarks of the system, that "Its morality pure and elevated, its religion entirely removed from the narrowness of sectarian bigotry, what parent is there, loving his children, and wishing to have them respected and happy, who would not desire that they should be educated under such a kind of moral and religious influence as has been described? Whether a believer in revelation or not, does he not know that without sound morals, there can be no happiness, and that there is no morality like the morality of the New Testament? Does he not know that without religion, the human heart can never be at rest, and that there is no religion like the religion of the Bible? Every well-informed man knows, that as a general fact, it is impossible to impress the obligations of morality with any efficiency on the heart of a child, or even on that of an adult, without an appeal to some mode which is sustained by the authority of God; and for what code will it be possible to claim this authority, if not for the code of the Bible?"

To very special inquiries addressed to him by Professor Stow, a distinguished Prussian teacher replied, "In Prussia, we have tried all sorts of ways; by extracts, by new translations, by commentaries written expressly for schools; but, after all these trials, there is now but one opinion among all acquainted with the subject, and that is, that the whole Bible, just as it stands in the translations in common use, should be a reading and recitation book in all the schools."

In regard to the relative importance of public teaching in the European monarchies and our republics, the Professor expresses his opinion thus:—"Republicanism can be maintained only by universal intelligence and virtue among the people, and disinterestedness and fidelity in the rulers. Republics are considered the natural foes to monarchies; and, when both start up side by side, it is taken for granted that one must supplant the other. Hence their watchful jealousy of each other. Now, when we see monarchies strengthening themselves by such a thorough system of education, secular and religious, as that we have described, are not republics warned to consider whether they are not exposed to double danger from vice and neglected education? And do not patriotism and the necessity of self-preservation call upon us to do more and better for the education of our whole people than any despotic sovereign can do for his? Did we stand alone—were there no rival governments on earth — or if we were surrounded by despotisms of degraded and ignorant slaves, like those of the ancient Oriental world — *even then,* without intelligence and religion in the great mass of the people, our liberties would soon be lost. How emphatically must this be the case *now,* when the whole aspect of things is changed, and monarchies have actually stolen a march upon republics in the promotion of sound education?"*

From "Thoughts on Popular Education in the United States," by a citizen of Pennsylvania, published in 1836, we take the following: — "Our object has been to show that all the children in our land deserve to be well and seasonably educated — they have a right to expect this at the hands of the governments under which they live, if they are to be held responsible for the discharge of duties of citizenship. No man can escape from responsibility in this matter. Under such institutions as ours, we stand

* Report of Professor E. C. Stow, to the General Assembly of Ohio, on "Elementary Public Instruction in Europe," made in 1837. Reprinted by order of the Legislature of Massachusetts, in 1838. Pages 9, 19, 53, 64.

too near to be independent of each other, or to be indifferent to each other's interests. Not a child can come to years of maturity, uneducated, without harm to us—to you—to the whole republic. The interest of each is the interest of all; and hence we argue the obvious and indispensable duty of every good man in the land to look narrowly into our institutions of public education, from the lowest to the highest, and do his full share of the labor of raising them to a proper elevation, and sustaining them there upon the pledge of fortune, honor, and even life itself."*

SECTION XV.

The responsibility of devising and carrying out the Policy of Religious Education in American Schools lies upon Christians.

THE policy of the people of the United States being, then, public education—universal education—Christian education—upon whom devolves the responsibility of carrying it into execution? We say it devolves upon the Christians of the United States. To whom else do multitudes, especially of the poor, look for the religious instruction of their children? Let the myriads of children in our Sunday schools answer. How many, who neglect all religious services themselves, gladly send their children to receive instruction which is exclusively religious? Would these people object to having their children instructed

* Frederick A. Packard.

in Christianity in the public schools? Would they not readily believe that the same religious zeal which sustained Sunday schools would be directed to the object of Christian instruction in the public schools, and would they not as readily approve it in one as the other? We believe the people of the United States are quite willing to entrust the religious instruction of their children to the Christians of the United States. We believe, further, that the duty of guiding, controlling, and enforcing this Christian instruction in our public schools, is one of the most important religious duties incumbent on the Christians of this country. It is a religious duty pressing upon Christians, not as Episcopalians, Methodists, Baptists, Congregationalists, or Presbyterians, but upon them as Christian citizens of the United States.

The character of the nation as a Christian country, is not derived from any one denomination of Christians, but from all; not from any feature which is peculiar to one, but from those great characteristics which distinguish them as a mass. It is this Christianity which is common to the prevailing denominations, which is to be communicated to and impressed upon the children of the United States in the public schools. The distinctive features of each denomination will grow soon enough and fast enough upon that soil which is common to all, under the special instructions of the family, the Sunday school, and the Church; and where these are wanting, as to a very large extent they are, it must be a consoling reflection to all true Christians, that no portion of the children of the country leave the public schools, without being made familiar with the Bible and its saving truths.

If Christians here do not choose to incur the responsibility of having Christ denied to the children in the public schools, they must overcome all denominational reluctance and engage heartily in this, the grandest duty of their position as republican Christians. Can any opportunity of preaching the gospel — of making known the way of life, be compared with that which is afforded by the public schools of the United States? And when we take into account the power which soon devolves upon the children, can any teaching be more influential than that which is aptly bestowed upon the advancing millions of our children? If, then, there is no legal, no constitutional obstacle in the way — as we trust we have shown there is not — of maintaining our character as a Christian people, by teaching Christianity in our national schools, can that denominational feeling which keeps Christians from this work have any affinity with Christianity? Can it be right for the men of any Church to say, if we cannot clothe the children with our uniform, we care not for their being clothed at all? Is it Christian-like to feed no lambs but those of our own fold, when all alike are His, who said, "Feed my lambs?" Nor is it any more excusable in a Church to withdraw wholly her countenance and co-operation from this work, in a vain effort to give a strictly denominational training to her own children. The narrowness of this view stands so strongly in contrast with the expansive scope of Christian love, that it needs only to be looked at to ensure condemnation. It can have its counterpart only, in the determination of the missionary to educate his own children and leave uncared for those of the heathen around him. The unchristian aspect of this policy is not its only unhappy feature. No large denomination of Christians can, by any organization in their power, accomplish the education of the whole number of children which would fall to their share. They could not probably reach more than a fifth of their own children, or at most a third.*

The remainder of the denominational lambs, and those especially who were children of the poor, must be left to run into the common fold: one portion of the children of a Church being educated upon one system and the residue upon another system. Now, if all received in the public schools the same course of religious instruction, each Church could readily make arrangements to furnish to its own children, upon some regular system, that special instruction deemed by it to be essential to complete the course of the public schools.

But if every separate denomination could reach the children of all its congregations and furnish them a good religious education, a vast multitude, exceeding probably two millions of children, would remain untaught, or taught in public schools over which, if they did not dwindle into utter inefficiency, little Christian sympathy would watch and no Christian wisdom would preside. Whilst, therefore, we would detract nothing from what can be done in the family,

---

* The Presbyterian Church has made efforts for several years to get up a general system of denominational education, with only about success enough to show the utter hopelessness of the attempt. The great mass of their own people cannot be reached by any denomination, however vigorous the attempt. — (*Appendix B.*)

in the Sunday school, in the Church, and in the numerous voluntary schools which special circumstances and feelings must ever create, we again aver that the great work of educating the millions remains to be accomplished by public means and public authority. And if a knowledge of Christianity is to be imparted to these millions, it can only be adequately done by the united, strenuous, intelligent and christian-like efforts of the chief religious denominations of the whole country. To stand aloof as a Church from this duty, involves a serious responsibility; to stand aloof from it as an individual, may involve not only a serious but a fatal responsibility. No thoughtful Christian can turn his back upon the religious welfare of the millions of children in the schools of this country, without hardening his heart and denying to his Christian affections and graces their proper scope and exercise.

We believe that the outward manifestations of Christianity do not keep up with the circumstances of the age in which we live, nor with its intelligence; and above all, they do not correspond to the opportunities and privileges of the land in which we live. In every age since the Christian era, and in every country, there have been circumstances, external or internal, in the condition of the people, which have prevented the free expansion and proper growth of Christianity. Sometimes it has been a defective ecclesiastical system, sometimes the repressive character of the temporal governments and the superstition or improper education of the people, but now at this day and in this country, the Christian — whether statesman, man of

9

science or philosopher — may look in what direction and pursue what line of inquiry, religious or social, he pleases, when he is considering how he can most promote the interests of Christianity and the temporal well-being of his fellow-men.

SECTION XVI.

Facilities enjoyed by Christians. — The doctrine of Christian Philanthropy. — Future triumphs of Christianity, where to be found.

At this day, then, and in this country, all pressure being taken from the mind and all undue restraint being removed from the tongue and pen — a favoring Providence having banished all obstacles to liberty of worship and the amelioration of human condition — we might hope for the most expansive and glorious exhibition of Christianity. A new development and a more rapid growth might be expected, where so much light is shed abroad and so many restrictions are removed. When we consider the summary of Christian duty, given by our Lord Himself — "Thou shalt love the Lord thy God with all thy heart and with all thy soul and with all thy mind," and "Thou shalt love thy neighbor as thyself" — we can readily comprehend, that in the past condition of humanity, the development of Christianity should rather be upon the first and great commandment than upon the second, which is like unto it. These commands being fundamental principles, any system built upon either must prove defective, as embracing one element when two were necessary. The obstacles to the expansion of Christian doctrine and the performance of Christian duty, lay chiefly in the way of the fulfilment of the second command. God, who is a spirit, and is not to be worshipped in this mountain or in that, nor yet at Jerusalem, could be worshipped in spirit and in truth in any circumstances and in every place; because this devotion could ascend from palace or from prison, and no human agency could wholly repress or stifle it. There has been, however, in all ages of Christianity, independent of the external difficulties in the way of a proper fulfilment of the second great commandment, a strong tendency to let religion run chiefly in the channel of the public service of God. We see this in grand and imposing rituals, in gorgeous Churches, in monkish seclusion on the one hand and in ecclesiastical magnificence on the other; we see many similar tendencies in the midst of Protestantism, but more especially in the vast fabric of theological science, the erection of which continues in our day.

In Papal countries the chief development of Christianity under this commandment to love our neighbor, was in the way of alms-giving; under Protestant rule it has been directed chiefly to the conversion of men, and to their spiritual welfare. It is now beginning to be understood, that mere alms-giving cannot be an adequate fulfilment of the love and duty we owe to our neighbor, not only because we owe this love and duty to those who do not require alms, but because that view does not cover the ground of our obligation; it is also plainly seen that mere efforts for the conversion of men, and for their spiritual welfare, however zealous and praiseworthy, do not comply with the whole scope and requirements of the command to love our neighbor as *ourselves*.

Protestants have failed hitherto in giving Christianity its due expansion on the side of philanthropy. No injunctions of the Bible are more urgent, and none are more frequently repeated, than those which relate to the duty of kindness to our fellow-men; the example of our Saviour, and his earnest exhortation to this duty, leave no room to evade the truth that humanity itself, in its broadest acceptation, is an essential and indispensable feature of Christianity. All religion is a mockery of God, if it does not include, in its scope and teaching, the well-being of men in this world, as well as the salvation of men in the world to come. Whatever advantage we seek for ourselves, whether it be of food or raiment, or good government or good education, we must be willing to impart to others according to our ability and opportunity. To be an intelligent Christian citizen of the United States, involves a consideration of every subject which concerns human advantage in this world, as well as what concerns the interests of men in the eternal world. By nothing less than this wide sweep of observation, can Christian men determine what is best for themselves, and best for their fellow-men; and by nothing less can their obligations be discharged. Where then we may again ask, for we have asked this question before, shall we find adequately developed the doctrine of Christian philanthropy? Where is the due application of Christianity to political economy to be found? Where the full bearing of Christianity upon social philosophy? We believe there is here then a whole department of Christian literature almost untouched, and certainly not begun to be elaborated as it deserves, and as the wants of the age urgently demand. The subject of Christian education in the public schools would, of course, fall within the scope of this elaboration of the social duties devolving upon citizens who are free to carry out the principles they profess. In that path of inquiry with the light of Divine Revelation upon every step, it would be very clearly seen what the Christian citizens of the United States owe to the children of the United States. In the proportion that Christianity is important to the temporal and eternal interests of these children, in that proportion is the obligation of those who have the power to impart it to them; in proportion as the fulfilment of this obligation is important to our national and State institutions, and through them to the cause of good government and human well-being throughout the world, in that proportion the Christians of this country by all means not inconsistent with our great law of toleration, are under obligation to imbue the rising generation with the great leading truths of Christianity. This is, perhaps, their greatest external duty, because it is pregnant with the richest results for Christianity and for human welfare in every aspect.

Hereafter the triumphs of Christianity should not be found or looked for in great hierarchies, or powerful ecclesiastical establishments, in grand cathedrals, in costly churches, in expensive and splendid rituals, in church blazonry, or even in denominational vastness; let us rather look for these triumphs, though the lines of differing opinions may never be obliterated, in the united efforts of Christians rising above their differences, and acting upon the common ground of their agreement, for the common good of the whole human family. When Christianity takes this aspect, and begins to work in this channel, the whole world will soon begin to admire; and all men will hasten to worship and adore Him who is the Author of such a system. Let us rather, hereafter, look for proofs of the spread of genuine Christianity, not to tall steeples and imposing architectural structures, but to the visible workings of sanctified human affections; which, being won over to Christ, are being exerted in every practicable direction, for the earthly and the heavenly interests of all that human family for which Christ suffered. Let us look for it in a system of religious training for the young, in Sunday schools and in public schools, which shall transcend all denominational limits as far as it surpasses all denominational power; let us look to see the visible influences of Christianity in every government where Christians can exercise a direct or indirect control; let us hope that these influences shall be so visible that they cannot be mistaken in the legislation and in the social institutions of every Christian nation; let us look to see the amelioration of human condition spreading co-extensively with the love and the light of the Gospel, that men may feel the warmth of Christian love in their bodies, while its light penetrates their souls. When Christianity has made this progress towards her perfect work, the rich will realize more clearly that they are stewards of Christ; the men of intellectual power and scientific acquisitions will realize better that they are responsible for these talents; the masses will be content, under such a system, to eat their bread in the sweat of their brows; the poor will feel assured that they are the chosen objects of Christian care, and the whole community will feel that one of the most pressing duties which rests upon them is to make sure that the laborer is not only hired, but that he receives a full reward of his labor.

All this, and far more, is within the scope of Christian love, acting under, and within the political institutions of the United States. All this mighty machinery of free government is but a combination of so many implements for the promotion of human welfare, placed under Christian influences, if not actually in Christian hands. The Christian men of this country may recoil and shrink from this responsibility, as unhappily they have been doing; but so long as they occupy their present position, they cannot escape them. It devolves upon them emphatically to maintain and improve our Constitutions, our laws, our social institutions; to sustain our great principles of Christian toleration and political compromise; to rectify and perfect our representative system; to purge and purify our elections; to banish corruption and ignorance from our Legislative bodies, and fill them with wiser, honester, and more patriotic men; to diffuse industry and secure its reward; to make Christian provision for the poor; and, finally, to devise and carry out that constantly-improving system of education by Sunday schools and public schools for the whole mass of our youth, which will fit them for the increasing responsibilities of those who are hereafter to determine the policy, and wield the destinies, of our constellation of republics.

APPENDIX A.

UNWILLING to distract the reader's attention by a longer digression on the Papacy, we resort for this purpose to the Appendix. Every man of letters, if not every man of reading, knows something of the Reverend Orestes A. Brownson, now simple O. A. Brownson, LL.D. His writings long since attracted our attention, for the sympathy displayed in them for the laboring classes. He has long enjoyed high repute as a scholar, and a man of ability. For a time he was charged with want of firmness of purpose and steadiness in his religious views. He has redeemed his character in that respect, for after changing his creed several times, he took refuge from his sea of doubts and turmoil of uncertainties, in the bosom of the Holy Roman Church, where he has been a fixture for some ten years. He possesses a high order of talent, but it consists chiefly in logical power. He grasps rapidly and firmly the relations of principles and ideas; his perceptions of these relations are clear, and his mode of expression is so transparent, that he can seldom be misunderstood. His attainments are large and varied; his memory is well stored with systems of faith and philosophy. His, however, is not the spirit nor the mind to grapple with the stern and ever-changing realities of this life. He does not like facts, they are too complicated and too stubborn for him, he can neither arrange nor manage them; he can neither detect nor expose their bearings nor relations. He does not judge the world nor its inhabitants by what it exhibits or what they do in any detail. One or two great facts at most are enough for his purpose, whilst he can swallow or emit any quantity of speculation. What his mind most craves is food for logic. The faith of Archimedes in the power of the lever, was not greater than that of O. A. Brownson in the power of logic. His good fortune, however, far exceeds that of the Syracusan mathematician, for the latter never found a place for his fulcrum, whilst the logician has discovered at length an illimitable field for his logic. He has found the Papacy—the Church of Rome, "the Holy Catholic Church, the Church of God, the Kingdom of Christ, the Immaculate Spouse of the Lamb, divinely commissioned and supernaturally assisted by the Holy Ghost, to teach and judge the law of God," "the Church a kingdom, the Kingdom of kingdoms, and Principality of principalities," God's vice-gerent on earth holding the keys of Heaven and Hell. Here are premises enough in this one idea of the Church, to satisfy the mind of the most morbidly gluttonous logician that ever wielded a pen. All that God can govern on earth, the Church can govern; the Church is supreme in spirituals, but as men must do all they do to the glory of God, as they must in all things yield implicit obedience to their spiritual superiors; therefore, the Church must take cognizance of all that is done under the sun. The Church must, in fact, take cognizance of all questions in morals and in politics, because there is no other infallible guide or criterion. The sweep of Mr. Brownson's logic covers the whole compass of God's wisdom, and the whole scope of his government on earth, for these are embraced in the theocracy of the Holy Catholic Church.

Allow Mr. Brownson this one stand-point of a divinely instituted Church as God's vice-gerent on earth, and then stand clear, or he will sweep you from your feet and carry you to heights and depths, only short, to use his own strong expression, "of nowhere." There certainly can be no imaginable thing done or conceived or expressed in this world, which Mr. Brownson cannot, from his point of view, prove to be religiously, temporally, properly and mentally, under the jurisdiction of the Holy Roman Church. If you attempt by any doubt, or caution or cavil to insinuate an objection, he will prostrate you as a profane person, an infidel denying all that is holy and pure and divine—as denying God himself in his Immaculate Spouse the Church.

With Mr. Brownson's really clear perceptions, with his skill in logical fence, he stands impregnable in his present position; and considering the character of his mind we see no way of dislodging him, for you might knock him heels over head a hundred times, and he would rise each time with not another idea in his head but Holy Roman Church. We see no method of meeting him, unless some crafty opponent should steal near enough to whisper in his ear, "God is great, and Mahomet is his Prophet." This fruitful idea, in its simple grandeur might be a sop for the most logical giant, or a tub for the hugest whale. For exhaustless as is his present theme, he has repeated some of his great lines of argument many times. On this new text he would enjoy not only as wide a scope, but he would be without a rival, past or present, for we much doubt if all the Muftis since the advent of Mahomet have, in their happiest and most ambitious moments, conceived what conclusions the logic of Mr. Brownson could draw from this pregnant phrase. He could on that simple expression build up a literature at once imposing, grand and comprehensive. Indeed, much of what he has written, would only need to be transferred into the language of the Turk or the Arab; for whatever may be predicated of the Holy Roman Church as in God's place on earth, might logically be predicated of Mahomet as the Prophet of God. The lack of infallibility might make a sad difference, for though there is scarcely any need, that is a stronghold to which Mr. Brownson often resorts, rioting as he does in his strength.

If Mr. Brownson cannot be coaxed down from his high position, we know not what better can be done, than to let him run his course until his breath fails him. No knight of the vizor and helmet was ever more rampant, more confident, or more proud; yet more discriminating than he of La Mancha, who would fight any thing on earth from a ghost to a wind-mill, he refuses the foemen that he deems not worthy of his steel. To a challenge for a discussion of the points between Protestants and the Hierarchy, given him at St. Louis recently, he replied:—

"I could not, permit me to say, consent to meet your chosen champion, in the way you propose, without in some measure compromising the rights of my religion, *conceding that the question between Catholics and Protestants is a debatable question*, and granting that Catholicity and Protestantism in some sense stand on the same level—a concession to heresy and error, and an indignity to truth, of which, I trust in God, I shall never be guilty." *

* And yet Mr. Brownson, in 1845, uttered this accusation: "Protestantism, afraid to meet the champions of the Cross in fair and open debate, conscious of her weakness and unskilfulness in argument, resorts to the civil arm to maintain her predominance." — *Brownson's Essays and Reviews*, 441.

This puts an end to this troublesome controversy without striking a blow.

There is another point of view from which the Papal career of Mr. Brownson may be regarded. Suspicious individuals have entertained the notion, that there were Jesuits and Priests in Protestant guise, in our highest places, making extraordinary pretensions of Protestant zeal and orthodoxy. We have never heard it suggested, that in return for these spies in our camp we have any in the conclaves of the Hierarchy. If there be any such, we might on strong grounds claim Mr. Brownson as our friend, and the most dangerous foe the Hierarchy has ever encountered. Until his advent as a defender of the Papacy and an expositor of its claims, a prudent, nay cautious reserve, was rigidly maintained. It seemed that the Papacy was really becoming Americanized; its odious features and inadmissible claims were kept very much out of sight; it appeared as if the Hierarchy were planting congregations here to fraternize as Christians with the Protestants around them. The Catholic people of this country have from the beginning shown this tendency. There has been no religious controversy here between Catholic people and Protestant people. Intelligent Protestants knew the spirit and ultimate designs of the Papacy, but the mass of the people, Catholic and Protestant, entertained no suspicion of the real nature and objects of the Hierarchy.

Such was the state of things when Mr. Brownson appeared on this stage. He changed the whole system of Papal tactics in this country, abandoning caution and throwing reserve to the winds. Clothed in the whole panoply of the Hierarchy, traditional, doctrinal, ritual, spiritual, temporal, he goes boldly before the public, announcing without hesitation and without disguise, plans, opinions and secrets hitherto buried deep among the mysteries of the priesthood. He virtually declares to the Hierarchy, if you hold the truth be not afraid of the light; if your Church is all it purports and claims to be, it cannot be known too soon; if there is no salvation out of your pale, let us call and force all men into it with the least delay possible; if no people, no government is safe, in any other than Papal hands, let us say so, that people may know it, and let us enter upon our dominion as soon as we can. Proceeding on these principles, he has opened up the councils of the Hierarchy with a boldness only to be matched by the disclosures he has made. No man in this country need now be ignorant of the claims or of the nature of the Papal Church. It is saying little for this exposition, that it surpasses any thing of the kind in the English language for clearness and frankness. There it is in Mr. Brownson's Review: the humblest reader can understand; let those whom it concerns profit by it!

But we must not indulge the idea that this exposition of Romanism is not the work of a sincere and an earnest, as well as able man. Educated in the American feeling of independence and openness, he carried these qualities into the Papal Church. He soon perceived they were hiding their light under a bushel; he brought it forth with an unfaltering hand, and placed it on a candlestick. He announced to his new friends, that they were too low and humble, living far below their privileges and position; that they were insensible to their present respectability and future destiny; that they had in the scheme of their Church a power which nothing could resist—a power embracing all terrestrial concerns, the title to which was indisputable, it being only a matter of time when it was to come into full exercise. He held up to their view the titles to this power, couched in such bold and commanding terms and set forth with such transcendent ability, that he carried the whole Hierarchy with him. His logical ability overcame all fear of consequences. They saw him take up their idea of the Church as the sole agent of God on the earth, and wielding it right and left, prostrate every opposing power, spiritual and temporal—crushing with equal ease republics and monarchies, sects and systems, literature and philosophy. With such a champion they adventured into the open field; it remains to be seen with what result.

The time is coming, and may not be very remote, when the pages of Brownson's Review shall be called as chief witnesses against the Hierarchy, when on trial at the bar of public opinion, for treason against the institutions of this country.

The Review can never be disowned by the Papal Priesthood, for it bears on its cover the *imprimatur* of two Arch-Bishops and twenty-three Bishops of the Romish Church in the United States. This is dated in May, 1849, at which time the character of the Review had fully developed itself; and after the Hierarchy had for several years watched the operation of the bolder policy upon which their neophyte had adventured. These ecclesiastics, knowing all this, felt "the propriety of encouraging him by their approbation and influence, to continue his literary labors in defence of the faith of which he has proved an able and intrepid advocate."

But this is not all. Mr. Brownson's name and works have travelled to the Spiritual Capital of the world. A Papal periodical, the *Correspondence de Rome*, gives a special notice of this Review. It regards the approval of the two Archbishops and twenty-three Bishops as "surpassing all eulogium." It notices "an extraordinary dissertation on the temporal power of the Church. We frankly confess that, to the best of our knowledge, no European writer has treated this question with more freedom and ability."

It is plain that the Hierarchy themselves did not fully appreciate the value of that vast Spiritual Corporation, of which they are the proprietors and managers, until the magnifying power of Mr. Brownson's logic was brought to bear upon it. Under the light of that instrument, it continues to swell in size, and develop in power, until all the world may soon be small enough, in comparison, to take refuge under its shadow.

There is abundant evidence in the pages of this Review, that its tone and doctrines are far from being so satisfactory to the Catholic laity. Some of these will be seen in the extracts which are to follow. On the occasion of commencing a new series of the Review, and on the last page of the number for January, 1853, he indulges in the following remarks and retrospection: —

"We have now, going on nine years, conducted this journal as a Catholic Review, and done so almost single-handed. We have spoken freely, frankly, boldly, we would hope not rashly, on all topics that have come up; and our aim has been to encourage a free, bold, and manly tone in our Catholic literature; to make Catholics feel that they are at home in this country, and need but courage in avowing, and fidelity in practising their religion, *to make the country Catholic*. . . . That we have disturbed many prejudices, trodden on a good many corns, and vexed not a few good souls, who would never have Catholicity speak above her breath, or in any but apologetic tones, is very likely. . . . As long as we can secure the approbation, and lose not the confidence of the *pastors* of the Church, we are content." — p. 136.

But we must not detain the reader longer from the following extracts from Mr. Brownson's Review. We have made our chief citations from the later numbers, supposing these to contain the best and most concentrated expression of the writer's views. We have made them longer than may appear needful, but we feared to do injustice by cutting them shorter. Long as they are, they convey but an imperfect presentation of the Reviewer's opinions, and very inadequate evidence of his ability. We heartily commend all who feel interested in the subject to the pages of the Review, in which they will find food for their profoundest reflections for many a day to come.

"They (the Protestants) cannot open our Review without finding something therein which shocks their sensibilities. Eternal damnation, with all its attendant and unnameable horrors, is forced upon their unwilling attention, as a thing which may be predicated of them, *in sensu composito*" (as a fixed fact), "with the same certainty which enables the by-stander to say of a man who has swallowed deadly poison, and who will not eject it, that he will surely die."—*April*, 1852, p. 166.

"The people have become either sovereign, or are aspiring after the sovereignty, and *one* sure sign that this new sovereign will fall into the pit into which kings and nobles fell is, that the people treat the Church as the kings and nobles treated her. Like the kings and the nobles in the ages of their revolt, the people are very tolerant of dead creeds, very intolerant of living Popes, practical Catholicity, and thronged confessionals. In speaking of the interference of ecclesiastics with secular affairs, as they call it, they use the same proud language which the sovereigns, their predecessors, the kings and nobles, once used. Poor people! They have mounted their tower, they have fixed their throne above the stars, they will be like the Most High! Poor people! they will fall,—they are falling; their *ignis fatuus* has led them to the precipice over which royalty and aristocracy fell. Ecclesiastical, regal, aristocratic, popular sovereignty,—the cycle is completed; will it begin again, or are we near the day of wrath which is to usher in the visible sovereignty of God over all flesh that has corrupted its way?"—*July*, 1852, pp. 405–6.

"So long as the free exercise of the Catholic religion meets with any obstacles, or finds any let or hindrance in any country, however free may be the sects or unbelievers, freedom of conscience is not secured, and the liberty of religion is not recognized and maintained."—Number 24, October, 1852, p. 445.

"No doubt, Mr. Bancroft understands by religious liberty, not the liberty of religion, freedom to believe what religion teaches and to practise what she commands, but the liberty of heresy and unbelief, the liberty to deny and blaspheme religion. But if he does, that is no reason why we should. The age in which we live no doubt agrees with him, but we are not obliged to err because the age errs. We do not consult the age in which we live in order to learn what is or is not truth. The freedom of religion is one thing, the freedom of heresy and unbelief is another, and we cannot fall into the gross folly of confounding the one with the other, because an heretical and unbelieving age, or an heretical or unbelieving historian, does. The two liberties are essentially distinct, and rest on very different grounds, and should never be confounded one with the other, or called by one and the same name. It is their confusion that creates the mischief, and gives to heretics the effrontery to call themselves the friends of religious liberty, and to pretend that the Church is a spiritual despotism. Religious liberty is the natural and inherent right of every man, for both by the natural and divine laws man has the right to render unto God what God requires of him,—the right to do his duty; but the liberty of heresy and unbelief is not a *natural* right, for by the law of nature, as well as the divine law, every man is bound to be of the true religion, and has no right to be of any other. All the rights the sects have or can have are derived from the state, and rest on expediency. As they have, in their character of sects hostile to true religion, no rights under the law of nature or the law of God, they are neither wronged nor deprived of liberty if the state refuses to grant them any rights at all; for wrong is done, liberty is taken away by the state, only when it violates rights which are held under the law of nature or the law of God, independent of the state, and which it is instituted not to concede, but to protect. The protection of the sects in the practice of their heresies is never on their side a question of right, or of what they may claim as a right, but is always a question of simple expediency; and so it must be, till you can obliterate all distinction between right and wrong, and establish the indifferency of truth and error. Heresy and unbelief, if really heresy and unbelief, are contrary to the law of God, and therefore have and can have no rights of their own, and then none that the state is, for their sake, bound to concede or to protect."—*Ibid*, pp. 455–6.

"We yield to no man in our devotion to religious liberty, but we have yet to learn that, in order to defend the liberty of religion, we must defend the equal liberty of heresy and unbelief, and maintain that the state is bound in all cases to place error and blasphemy on an equal footing with truth and piety."—*Ibid*, p. 457.

In arguing against the position of the Gallican Church, in which by agreement the Church and the State hold their power directly from God, the Reviewer sums up his argument thus:

"If in spirituals Peter could say to Cæsar, 'I am your master,' in temporals Cæsar could say to Peter, 'I am your lord, and you are my subject.' To this specious theory, which is still popular even with many Catholics, there are one or two rather grave objections. In the first place, the normal relation of the two orders is not, and cannot be, that of equality or mutual independence, because the temporal order, as we have heretofore shown, exists for the spiritual, not for itself, and is therefore subordinate to the spiritual, and consequently subject to the spiritual sovereign, in obedience to whose authority the temporal sovereign must govern. This lies in the nature of the case, and cannot be denied, if we concede any spiritual order at all."—*July*, 1853, p. 290.

"There is always, even in the most Catholic times and in the most Catholic states, a party, more or less numerous, who have no conception of religion as law, or of the Church as a kingdom, with a constitution, laws, and chiefs of her own, set up on the earth with plenary authority, under God, over states and individuals, — a party who never think of the Church as a divinely constituted government, even in spirituals, and count for nothing her external organition, her mission, or her discipline. The Creed, the Sacraments, and the Ritual compromise, for them, the whole of religion, and they never can or never will understand why these may not be just as salutary when held out of unity as when held in it."—*Ibid*, p. 299.

There is, indeed, a large party in the bosom of the Catholic Church, who believe that Protestants will not all perish forever. Just as Protestants believe that every truly pious person in the Catholic Church will be saved, in spite of the sins of the Hierarchy.

"In these revolutionary times the great point to be specially insisted on, it seems to us, is, that the Church is a government, a kingdom, the Kingdom of kingdoms and Principality of principalities. What is most important is, to understand that she is a power, an organized power, divinely constituted, assisted, and protected, representing the Divine authority on earth, and as such universal and supreme. How the state is organized, or by whom administered, is a matter of comparative indifference. The state may be monarchical or republican, aristocratic or democratic, if it only be understood and conceded that over it, as over every individual, there is a spiritual kingdom, a spiritual authority, commissioned by God himself, to interpret and apply his law to every department of human life, individual or social, public or private; for if such authority be recognized and submitted to, no interest, temporal or spiritual, can fail to be protected and promoted. Undoubtedly, the assertion of this authority is a delicate matter, owing to the utter confusion which obtains in men's minds respecting it; but we pray such of our readers as have some little candor and good-will to bear in mind that to assert this authority is by no means to merge the state in the Church, or to claim for the Church direct temporal authority, although even to claim for her direct temporal authority is not, to say the least, forbidden to the Catholic. What we here assert is, that the spiritual authority, in the nature of the case and by the express appointment of God, extends beyond what are ordinarily called spirituals, — to all matters which do or can interest conscience, or concerning which there can arise any question of right or wrong, true or false. The Church, we grant, nay, maintain, is spiritual, and governs in reference, and only in reference, to a spiritual end; but as the temporal order subsists only by and for the spiritual, she, though not it any more than God is the world, nor the temporal authority itself, has, as the God whose representative on earth she is, supreme authority over it, and the full right, under God, to prescribe to it the law it is bound in all things and at all times to consult and obey." — *Ibid*, p. 300.

"There is a point beyond which submission to the temporal authority, whether monarchical or republican, aristocratic or democratic, is apostasy, and can in no sense whatever be tolerated. We must say all this, and our enemies know it; and they know that the great body of the faithful will place that point where it is declared to be by the Sovereign Pontiff."—*Ibid*, p. 314.

"The leading political doctrine of the day, democracy itself as now generally understood, is only the political phase of Calvinism, and it wants little of being pure socialism, for it excludes God, and renders society supreme. In fact socialism is nothing but Protestantism gone to seed, and no man can be a consistent Protestant without holding all the principles necessary to serve as the logical basis socialism. None, therefore, but a Catholic, as we so often repeat, can either consistently or successfully attack the socialistic tendencies of the country."—*Ibid*, p. 415.

"It is a grave mistake to suppose that all is Catholic in Catholic countries, and that the Church there has every thing her own way. Scarcely a professedly Catholic government, from the first Christian Emperor down to the last of the German Kaisers, or to the present Emperor of the French, has left the Church perfectly free to enforce in her own way her own discipline, and has been ready in all things to lend her, when requisite, the support, for that purpose, of the secular arm. As a general thing, professedly Catholic governments, as well as others, have shown themselves at all times jealous of the ecclesiastical authority, and sought to treat ecclesiastics officiating in their respective dominions as subject to their jurisdiction. They never willingly recognize the Church as the kingdom of God on earth, independent of all earthly kingdoms, and above them all, instituted for the express purpose of making the kingdoms of this world the kingdoms of God and of his Christ, — of teaching and directing all men and nations in the way of holiness. Even when they cheerfully admit her as doctrine and as worship, they only reluctantly recognize her as a kingdom, as government, as law. They claim to be themselves, each in its own dominions, the supreme and only government, and hence, when the Church presents herself in the aspect of a government, and of a government that claims to govern not only abstractions, rites, and ceremonies, but men, and men, too, in every department of life, in their souls as well as their bodies, in their relations to earth as well as to heaven, to their temporal rulers as well as to their spiritual chiefs, she seems to them a dangerous rival, and they place themselves on their guard against her, and seek to deprive her of her governing power, and to confine her action to a subordinate sphere. This would be well enough, if the secular government were, as it assumes to be, the supreme and only government, if God had nothing to do with the temporal order, or if it had pleased him to intervene in the government of mankind only through the medium of the state; that is, if the state, and not the Church, were the kingdom of God on earth. It would also be well enough, if the Church were a mere human institution, and not, as she is, the Church of God, divinely constituted and commissioned for the very purpose of teaching and applying to sovereigns as well as to subjects, and to sovereigns in their public and official capacity as well as in their private capacity, the supreme law, the law which all alike, and in all things, are bound to obey."] — *April*, 1853, p. 152.

"We cannot name a single professedly Catholic state, that has afforded, for these three hundred years, more than a momentary consolation to the Holy Father. The bitterest enemies of the Holy Father have been of his own household, and the only sovereigns in the eighteenth century, and the first half of the nineteenth, that treated him with respect, were, we grieve to say it, sovereigns separated from his communion. Pius the Seventh was indebted to Great Britain, Russia, and Prussia, for the restoration of the temporal possessions of the Holy See, usurped by one Catholic Emperor and retained by another. How absurd, then, to suppose that all in Catholic states is Catholic, that even professedly Catholic sovereigns are always, or even ordinarily, the obedient sons of the Church, and that she is responsible for all that is done in countries where she is legally recognized!

"We have, as Catholics, not a few grievances to complain of in this country, but there is no Catholic country in the world where the Church is as free and as independent as she is here, none where the Pope is so truly Pope, and finds, so far as Catholics are concerned, so little resistance to the full exercise of his authority as visible Head of the Church. The reason is, not that the government here favors or protects the Church, but that it lets her alone."] — *Ibid.* p. 154–5.

These two passages furnish evidence of the breadth of the Papal claims for secular power, and prove also that even where the population and rulers were Catholic, there has been a constant resistance to this claim. Eels do not always become so used to skinning that they do not occasionally squirm under the process.

"Discipline belongs to the Church as much as doctrine, and she bears the keys as well as the word, and her liberty is as much infringed when she is denied the liberty of exercising the power of the keys, as when she is denied the liberty of teaching, or of celebrating Mass. She has authority over all persons, whatever their state or dignity, to bind and loose, and God assures her that whatever she binds or looses on earth, shall be bound and loosed in heaven. This power is that which constitutes her a kingdom, and gives her the faculty to govern. Without it she might teach and pray, and advise, but could have no power to make her doctrines observed or her precepts obeyed. To deprive her of this power, to prohibit her from fulminating spiritual censures, and binding the violator of God's law, whoever he may be, would be to reduce her to the level of a sect or of a school of philosophy; and to resist the exercise of this terrible power is no less sinful than to deny the truth she teaches. It is by this power especially that she is able to enforce the obedience of subjects to their sovereigns, and the practice of justice by sovereigns to their subjects, and therefore it is only by recognizing this power, and allowing her free scope for its effectual assertion, that she can exercise that guardian care of the state, and have that conservative influence in society, which late events have proved to be so indispensable.

"This granted, it is easy to see the wisdom and necessity of the Papal constitution of the Church. The Church is a kingdom, a power, and as such must have, if she is to exercise her authority, a supreme chief. This authority is to be exercised over states as well as over individuals; therefore the Church as a government must be Catholic, for otherwise it could not govern all nations; it must be one and Catholic, otherwise it would be subjected by each sovereign in his own dominions. And this unity and Catholicity are impossible without the monarchical constitution, without its subjection to a single head, with supreme authority over the whole body, prepared at any moment to exercise that authority on any point and against any enemy that may be necessary. This is the point towards which we have been looking from the first, and contains the practical lesson which we wish to impress on the minds of our readers. The Church is built on Peter, and its defence is all included in the defence of Peter, as the state is defended in defending its sovereign. *Ubi Petrus, ibi Ecclesia.* But though we have reached the point at which we have been aiming, we must reserve its development and defence to a future number." —*Ibid.* p. 162–3.

"Protestantism, and through it its father, the Devil, gains *souls.* Provided he gains these, think you he cares whether they come to him by formal apostacy, or by the breach of a commandment, be it the fourth or the sixth? He gets them at any rate."—*Ibid.* p. 248.

"It is not our purpose, in this article, to argue the point between radicalism and Christian politics. We have often discussed it, and shall often discuss it again in our pages. Our present purpose is to cite decisions of positive law, and to put two or three questions. One is, whether there is any divine law which convicts modern democracy of sin. Another is, what sort of a sin is it? Finally, whether Catholics in our country have been, are, or may be tempted to commit it. It is clear enough, if religion be supreme over politics, as it certainly is, — if modern radical doctrines be at variance with the fourth commandment, as they certainly are, — if this fourth commandment be yet binding upon the conscience of men, as nobody can deny, and if its breach incurs the penalty of eternal damnation, as it certainly does, — that notwithstanding the outcry of baptized and unbaptized radicals, the sin must be placed in the same category with murder, theft, and lust." —*Ibid.* p. 252.

If the writer has any antipathy stronger than that against Protestantism, it is his hatred of Democracy.

"It is quite the fashion even for Catholic politicians to assert that, though the Church is supreme in spirituals, the State in temporals is absolutely independent of her authority. 'Render unto Cæsar the things that are Cæsar's. As long as the Church keeps within her own province, and confines herself to spirituals, we respect her, and submit to her authority; in spirituals, we even recognize the authority of the Pope, and allow that in them he may do what he pleases; but he has no authority in temporals, and in them we will do as we please.' Such is the popular doctrine of the day, and of not a few who would take it as a gross affront and as downright injustice were we to insinuate that they are but sorry Catholics. Scarcely a Catholic amongst us engaged in politics can open his mouth without uttering this doctrine, and uttering it as if it were an incontestable truth and a maxim of divine wisdom. It has become the commonplace of the whole political world, and is rung out upon us from thrones and the cabinets of ministers, the halls of justice and legislation, and from the hustings and the caucus. Whoso ventures to question it, is stared at as the ghost of some old dreamy monk of the Dark Ages. Let us, then, be allowed to examine it."—*January*, 1853, p. 34.

The reviewer proceeds to the examination. He allows no distinction between a monarchy and a democracy. "You only crown the people instead of one man." His conclusion is thus stated:

"We wish the people free, — free from their own passions, and from yours and mine,—alike free from despots and from demagogues; and we know there is and can be no freedom for them, either in spirituals or temporals, except in so far as they are subjected to the law of God, as interpreted and applied by his Church."—*Ibid.* p. 37.

"No man, unless a downright atheist, dares, in just so many words, to assert the monstrous proposition, that the temporal order is not subjected to the law of God."—*Ibid.* p. 38.

"This established, we demand to whom, under God, it belongs to keep, interpret, and declare the law of Christ? Whom hath our Lord constituted the depositary, the guardian, and the judge of his law? Certainly the Holy Roman Catholic and Apostolic Church, and the successor of Peter as visible head or supreme chief of that Church. . . . . The commission is to the Church, not to the State, and nowhere can it be found that our Lord has made princes, as such, guardians and judges of his law, even in the temporal order. He only gives them authority to execute it when declared to them. Besides, to keep, teach, and declare the law of Christ, whether in spirituals or temporals, is manifestly a spiritual function, and temporal sovereigns, it is confessed in the very doctrine we oppose, have no spiritual functions."—*Ibid.* 41.

"All things are ordered in reference to her (the Church). Her Maker is her Husband, and he will own none as his children who have not been carried in her womb and nursed at her breasts. Such is his will, eternal as his own being, and which is without variableness or shadow of turning, immutable and immovable as his own nature. She has been instituted expressly to guide, assist, and conduct us to God. For this end she has been made the depository of the law of Christ, authorized to keep, to teach, to interpret and apply it,—to teach, feed, rule, and defend all men and nations, in reference to their final and only end. How, then, say she has no authority over temporals? How can she have authority to judge the only end for which temporals exist, or have any right to exist, if she have not the right to judge them, and to approve or condemn them as they do or do not subserve this end. How can she have charge of the end without also having charge of the means, since the means are necessarily subordinated to the end, and controlled by it? As she has charge of the end, that is, of gaining the end, she must have charge of the means, and as the temporal exists only as a means to man's final end, she must, by virtue of the very spiritual authority which she confessedly is, have supreme power over the temporal, and plenary authority to govern it according to the demands or the utility of the end, and therefore in all respects whatever."—*Ibid.* 46.

"Now, although we do not say that the Church commissions the State, or imposes the conditions on which it holds its right to govern, yet as it holds under the law of Christ, and on conditions imposed by that law, we do say that she, as the guardian and judge of that law, must have the power to take cognizance of the State, and to judge whether it does or does not conform to the conditions of its trust, and to pronounce sentence accordingly; which sentence ought to have immediate practical execution in the temporal order, and the temporal power that resists it is not only faithless to its trust, but guilty of direct rebellion against God, the only real Sovereign, Fountain of all law, and Source of all rights, in the temporal order as in the spiritual."—*Ibid.* 47.

"The Pope, then, even by virtue of his spiritual authority, has the power to judge all temporal questions, if not precisely as temporal, yet as spiritual,—for all temporal questions are to be decided by their relation to the spiritual,—and therefore has the right to pronounce sentence of deposition against any sovereign when required by the good of the spiritual order."—*Ibid.* 48.

"If the Church is the spiritual power, with the right to declare the law of Christ for all men and nations, can any act of the State in contravention of her canons be regarded as a law? The most vulgar common sense answers that it cannot. Tell us then, even supposing the Church to have only spiritual power, what question can come up between man and man, between sovereign and sovereign, between subject and sovereign, or sovereign and subject, that does not come within the legitimate jurisdiction of the Church, and on which she has not by divine right the power to pronounce a judicial sentence? None? Then the power she exercised over sovereigns in the Middle Ages was not a usurpation, was not derived from the concession of princes or the consent of the people, but was and is hers by divine right; and whoso resists it rebels against the King of kings and Lord of lords. This is the ground on which we defend the power exercised over sovereigns by Popes and Councils in the Middle Ages.

"We know this ground is not acceptable to sovereigns, to courtiers, or to demagogues. But is that our fault? Who has made it our duty to please them? Are we not bound to please God, and to adhere to the truth, let it offend whom it may?"—*Ibid.* 49.

We have in the United States a vast body of Constitutional and Legislative enactments which are in flat contravention of the Canon Law. "The most vulgar (Papal) common sense" pronounces all these to be void. The Papal ecclesiastic laughs in his sleeve, and says "wait a little," and we will show you what such nonsense is worth!

"The modern demagogue does for the people what the German lawyer did for the German Kaiser. He does not say the people are sovereign under the law of God interpreted by the Church; but he says the people are the living law, the fountain of all rights, and from them emanates all just authority, both civil and ecclesiastical. Therefore he makes the people emperor, sovereign pontiff, god. Hence he actually uses the strange terms people-king, people-pontiff, people-god. Read Pierre Leroux, read Giuseppe Mazzini, and you will find these barbarous epithets, or their equivalents, used in sober earnestness, and the last-mentioned of these worthies is the recognized chief of the whole European democracy, and commands the sympathy of constitutional England and democratic America. The people are crowned and deified in opposition to kings and emperors, but it is still the assertion of the independence, nay, the supremacy, of the temporal order, and the denial of its subordination to the law of God. The people are king, pope, god, and may do what they will, and hence for the despotism of kings we have the despotism of the mass, social despotism, or rather the despotism of the demagogues who control the people.

"But some revolt, again, at this, and will no more submit to king-people than to any other king. They see in the people only a collection of individuals, and will not admit of the whole collectively any more than is true of each individual taken separately. Hence we actually hear individuals, not in a mad-house, not looked upon as out of their senses, but honored and held up as the great lights of their age, claim for each individual what the lawyers claimed for Kaiser, what the demagogue claims for the people *en masse*, and assert, each for himself, I am emperor, sovereign pontiff, and god. It is only the logical consequence of the Protestant doctrine of private judgment, only Protestantism consistently developed. But with this monstrous claim of the individual, no law, no government, no society, nothing but anarchy, is possible. Here is where the movement against the absolutism of kings does and must end. Asserting the independence of the temporal order, it passed on to the absolutism of the mass, and from that it passes on to the absolutism of the individual, the Free Trade of the late William Leggett, and would pass further, only there is no further; sink to a lower deep, only a lower deep there is not.

"Would you have us follow in this track, assert people-king, people-pontiff, people-god, or declare each individual emperor, supreme pontiff, god? Would you have us, in order not to incur the censure of our age, or offend the god of our demagogues, so belie our common sense, so stultify ourselves, as to accept such arrant nonsense, or rather such horrid blasphemy, which the fools of the day boast as a proof of the light and progress of this nineteenth century? But we must do it, or reassert the Catholic doctrine of the supremacy of the spiritual order, and maintain that the whole temporal order in all things is subordinated to the law of God as interpreted by the Roman Catholic Church."—*Ibid.*, pp. 56, 57.

"The Church any day is as sovereign as Cæsar, and as safe a depository of power, and the insolence and encroachments of Churchmen, suppose them to be as great as the most shameless courtier or politician ever pretended, are less intolerable than the insolence and encroachments of Cæsar and his satellites. Any day the mitre is above the crown, and the priest above the demagogue. But after all, we have a tolerable pledge of the good behavior, of the justice and discretion, of the Church in the fact that she is the Holy Catholic Church, the Church of God, the Kingdom of Christ, the immaculate Spouse of the Lamb, divinely commissioned and supernaturally assisted by the Holy Ghost to teach and judge the law of God, and to conduct individuals and nations in the way of truth and holiness. We trust her in all that concerns the soul, and it would be a hard case if we could not trust her also in all that concerns the body."—*Ibid.* pp. 58, 59.

"When, then, we find a sovereign pontiff judging, condemning, and deposing a secular prince, releasing his subjects from their obligation to obey him, and authorizing them to choose them another king, we may regret the necessity for such extreme measures on the part of the Pontiff, but we see in them only the bold and decided exercise of the legitimate authority of the spiritual power over the temporal; and instead of blushing for the chief of our religion, or joining our voice to swell the clamor against him, we thank him with our whole heart for his fidelity to Christ, and we give him the highest honor that we can give to a true servant of God and benefactor of mankind."—*Ibid.* 61.

"O Sovereign Pontiff, Successor of the Prince of the Apostles, Vicar of God on earth, if ever through love of the world, or through fear of the secular power, whether royal or popular in its constitution, I forget to assert thy rights as supreme chief under Christ, my Saviour, of the whole spiritual order, and as such supreme alike in spirituals and in temporals, let my right hand forget her cunning, and my tongue cleave to the roof of my mouth!

"We yield to none in our loyalty to civil government, and we are loyal to it because we are loyal to the successor of Peter. Religion with us governs politics, and the Pope is lord of Cæsar. Without the Pope, the Church would break into fragments, and dwindle into puny and contemptible Protestant sects; without the Church, religion would become an idle speculation, a maudlin sentiment, or a loathsome superstition."—*Ibid.* 62.

"No matter what may be the self-complacency of Protestants, the lofty airs they assume, the great, swelling words they use, or the grave tones in which they speak of their pure, unadulterated evangelical religion, the fact is, Protestantism, considered in itself, is not and never was a religion, true or false, never had a single religious element, never was sought and has never been upheld from any strictly religious motives."—*Ibid.* p. 89.

This is endorsed by two Arch-Bishops and twenty-two Bishops, for their *imprimatur* is on the cover of the Review which contains the above. Let it not excite the ire of any thin-skinned Protestant. It is a regular step in a process of sound logic, in which the only error is in the premises. Let any man but admit the Catholic idea of the Church, and he will find himself drawn, by the power of logic, to the same conclusion. It is only because some who use this phrase do not ride their logic so hard, that they are not carried at once to the repose of the Church of Rome.

"The men who adhere to Protestantism, if they ever investigate their own motives, know perfectly well that they adhere to it only because it emancipates them from all religion, by subjecting religion now to the State and now to the individual judgment or caprice.

. . . . "The Reformation in principle was not an attempt, though a mistaken or an unlawful attempt, to get a purer and better religion than the Catholic; it was simply a rebellion against God, prompted by the flesh, incited by the Devil. It was born of hell, and hence it is that we seldom affect or disturb it by refuting its heresies. . . . . We must oppose Protestantism, not as a false theology, but as a revolt of the flesh against God, — as the mad attempt of men to set themselves up above their Maker, and to live as they list.

"No doubt many Catholics will think this too severe, but it is because we apprehend that there are some who will so think that we say it. We wish our friends to be fully aware of the enormity of Protestantism. We are not wholly ignorant of the infinite tenderness of the Gospel, and we can admire, as well as others, the beauty of Christian charity. We know, too, that many, very many, Protestants are amiable in their social relations, are faithful to their engagements, and honest in their dealings, and so far very superior to their Protestantism itself; but not therefore are we to confound their purely human or Gentile virtues with the supernatural virtues of the true Christian. We know what allowances also to make for ignorance and for prejudices early instilled in the minds of Protestants; but we are speaking to Catholics, who are always in danger of thinking too favorably of those who are involved in the Protestant rebellion against God. We have no wish to be severe; we speak not in wrath; we would willingly lay down our life to bring Protestants into the Church of God; but we believe it true kindness, true charity, to strip off the mask from Protestantism, to expose its real features, and to compel it to bear its own appropriate name, so that all the world may see that there is no medium between Catholicity and no religion, any more than there is between virtue and vice, truth and falsehood, Christ and the Devil. If this offends, then let it offend; if it do not offend God, we shall remain at our ease."—*Ibid.* pp. 110, 111.

On the same page from which the last passage is taken we have the quotation, "*Quem Deus vult perdere, prius dementat.*" This furnishes the key to the extraordinary frankness of this American Romanist. It is scarcely possible to draw any other inference than that he wishes to precipitate conclusions with Protestants. Goliah himself could not be bolder, nor provoke a combat in more stinging taunts or denunciations.

"Written Constitutions, parliamentary bodies, all the contrivances of human wit and wisdom to restrict the power of the ruler, or to bind the subject to obedience, are of themselves insufficient to maintain authority against anarchy, or liberty against despotism. The legitimate authority of the prince, and the just liberty of the subject, wrangle as you will, are practicable only under the supremacy of a divinely instituted and supernaturally assisted and protected Church. To enslave this Church, or not to recognize her authority and secure her freedom and independence of action, is at once to destroy the authority of the prince and the liberty of the subject, or to convert authority into despotism and liberty into license."—*Ibid.* p. 132.

We subjoin some shorter but not less significant passages, from the pages of a volume of "Reviews and Essays," published by Mr.

Brownson, in 1852. There are selections by himself from his previous productions of such articles as he deemed most important, and such as he desired most to keep before the public. We commend this volume to Protestant readers. It is not soporific, but contains enough to keep the faculty of wonder awake in those who have not, as Mr. Webster once alleged to be his case, had it worn out by too constant use.

"The Professor contends that the Church is hostile to civil government; we would respectfully ask him if he has reflected, that, without her, civil government becomes impracticable. How, without her as umpire between government and government, and between prince and subject, and without her as a spiritual authority to command the obedience of the subject and the justice of the prince, will he be able to secure the independence of nations, and wise and just government."—*Brownson's Essays and Reviews*, p. 207.

"Our own government is sustained solely by the accidental advantages of the country, consisting chiefly in our vast quantities of unoccupied fertile lands, which absorb our rapidly increasing population, and form a sort of safety-valve for its superfluous energy. Strip us of these lands, or let them be filled up so that our expanding population should find its limit, and be compelled to recoil upon itself, our institutions would not stand a week."—*Ibid.* p. 208.

"In submitting to her (the Church of Rome) we are free, because we are submitting to God, who is our rightful sovereign, to whom we belong, all that we have, and all that we are. Freedom is not in being held to no obedience, but in being held to obey only the legal sovereign; and the more unqualified the obedience, the freer we are. Perfect freedom is in having no will of our own, in willing only what our sovereign wills, and because he wills it. If the Church, as we cannot doubt, be really commissioned by God, the more absolute her authority, the more unqualified our submission, the more perfect is our liberty, as every man knows, who knows any thing at all of that freedom wherewith the Son makes us free. But in yielding obedience to a Protestant sect, it is not the same. When any one of our sects undertakes to dictate to conscience, it is tyranny; because, by its own confession, it has received no authority from God. It is tyranny, even though what it attempts to enforce be really God's word; for it attempts to enforce it by a *human*, and not by a *divine* authority. It would still tyrannize, because it has no right to enforce any thing at all. It may say, as our sects do say, it has the Bible, that the Bible is God's word, and that it only exacts the obedience to God's commands which no man has the right to withhold. Be it so. But who has made it the keeper and executor of God's laws? Where is its commission under the hand and seal of the Almighty?"—*Ibid.* pp. 220–1.

"We, as Catholics, are taught by a divinely authorized Teacher, that government is the ordinance of God, and that we are to respect and obey it as such in all things not repugnant to the law of God; and we have an authority higher than its, higher than our own, to tell us, without error, or the possibility of error, — because by Divine assistance and protection rendered infallible, — when the acts of government conflict with the law of God, and it becomes our duty to resist the former in obedience to the latter."—*Ibid.* p. 361.

"We have always a public authority, which, as it is inerrable, can never be oppressive, to guide and direct us, and if we resist the civil law, it is only in obedience to a higher law, clearly and distinctly declared by a public authority higher than the individual, and higher than the state."—*Ibid.* p. 362.

"We have spoken of the tendency, under the name of liberty, to anarchy and license; but there is another tendency, under the pretext of authority, to civil despotism, or what has been very properly denominated *Statolatry*, or the worship of the state, that is, elevating the state above the Church, and putting it in the place of God. Both tendencies have the same origin, that is, in the Protestant rejection of the spiritual authority of the Church on the one hand, and the assertion of private judgment on the other; and in fact, both are but the opposite phases or poles of one and the same principle." — *Ibid.* p. 363.

"She (the Papal Church) is an integral, an essential element in the constitution of society, and it is madness and folly to think of managing it and securing its well-being without her. She is the solution of all difficulties, and without her none are solvable." — *Ibid.* p. 365.

"For on the Catholic population, under God, depend the future destinies of these United States. The principles of our holy religion, the prayers of our Church, and the fidelity to their trusts of the Catholic portion of the people, are the only sure reliance left us."—*Ibid.* p. 367.

"It is evident, from these considerations, that Protestantism is not and cannot be the religion to sustain democracy; because, take it in which stage you will, it, like democracy itself, is subject to the control of the people, and must command and teach what they say, and of course must follow, instead of controlling, their passions, interests, and caprices."—*Ibid.* 375, 376.

"The Constitution, as a restraint on the will of the people or the governing majority, is already a dead letter. It answers to talk about, to declaim about, in electioneering speeches, and even as a theme of newspaper leaders, and political essays in reviews; but its effective power is a morning vapor after the sun is well up."—*Ibid.* 377.

"The Constitution is practically abolished, and our government is virtually, to all intents and purposes, as we have said, a pure democracy, with nothing to prevent it from obeying the interest or interests which for the time being can succeed in commanding it."—*Ibid.* p. 378.

"And this is good proof of our position, that Protestantism cannot govern the people, — for they govern it, — and therefore that Protestantism is not the religion wanted; for it is precisely a religion that can and will govern the people,—be their master,—that we need.

"If Protestantism will not answer the purpose, what religion will? The Roman Catholic, or none. The Roman Catholic religion assumes, as its point of departure, that it is instituted, not to be taken care of by the people, but to take care of the people; not to be governed by them, but to govern them. The word is harsh in democratic ears, we admit; but it is not the office of religion to say soft or pleasing words. It must speak the truth even in unwilling ears, and it has few truths that are not harsh and grating to the worldly-minded or the depraved heart. The people need governing, and must be governed, or nothing but anarchy and destruction await them. They must have a master."—*Ibid.* pp. 379, 380.

"But it needs no very sharp observation to perceive that our Republic has virtually failed to accomplish the hopes of its founders, and that it is, without some notable change in the people, destined either to a speedy dissolution, or to sink into a miserable timocracy, infinitely worse than the most absolute despotism. Protestantism, if it could originate, has not proved itself able to sustain it."—*Ibid.* 433.

"Here is our hope for our Republic. We look for our safety to the spread of Catholicity. We render solid and imperishable our free institutions just in proportion as we extend the kingdom of God among our people, and establish in their hearts the reign of justice and charity. And here, then, is our answer to those who tell us Catholicity is incompatible with free institutions. *We tell them that they cannot maintain free institutions without it.* It is not a free government that makes a free people, but a free people that makes a free government; and we know no freedom but that wherewith the Son makes free."—*Ibid.* 441.

We are certainly under no small obligations to Mr. Brownson, for the very thorough and effective manner in which he has stripped the Papacy of the many disguises it has worn, not only here, but elsewhere. We mistake very much if his revelations do not gain him more credit among the public authorities of Europe than among those of the United States. No ecclesiastic in this country has had the frankness, much less the courage, to do what he has done. He has presented the Romish system, in all its magnitude, as a veritable rival to our own. He is thoroughly satisfied that our systems of government have failed, root and branch. He tells us that, but for our vast fund of public lands, "our institutions would not last a week;" "that we want the moral elements, without which a republic cannot stand;" that we "have really no social bond, no true patriotism;" "that there can be no common moral culture in the country,—no true religious training;" that some already pronounce "this republicanism a mere delusion;" and he avers that, "if the country remains Protestant fifty years longer, facts will prove it;" he tells us that "Protestantism never has produced, and never can produce, the virtues, without which a republican government can have no solid foundation;" "that the tendency of Protestantism is to reproduce heathen antiquity, with all its cant, hollowness, hypocrisy, slavery, and wretchedness;" that "Protestantism may seem, by its principle of private judgment, to favor civil freedom; it often attempts to establish free popular institutions, but it wants virtue to sustain them;" that you may "turn Protestantism over, and analyze it as you will, you can make nothing of it but vulgar pride;" "a moral disease, rather than an intellectual aberration;" "the wrongness of the head being the cause of the rottenness of the heart;" "that human pride, just now, takes the form of Socialism, and Socialism is the Protestantism of our times;" and that, for all this, the only remedy is in the Papal Church. We cannot wonder that men who entertain such views as the above extracts exhibit, should be in a haste to extirpate so poisonous a pestilence as Protestantism. Let it not be said that these two great religious parties are merely abusing each other, and that it is of little consequence what they say. If it were a mere question of hard names, or severe speeches, it would, indeed, be of little import, except for the disgrace of the strife. The dispute is, however, to be ultimately one of vital moment to the peace of the country, and perhaps to its prolonged existence as a republic. The great question now presented to the people of the United States, and, thanks to Mr. Brownson, presented without disguise, is this:—Shall we persist in carrying on our present republican institutions, with liberty of worship and the right of private judgment, or shall we confess that our experiment has failed, and stand ready to accept the protection and guidance of the infallible Church?—That is the important question now pending—if not extremely pressing at this moment, it is becoming more so every day, by our neglect.

It is not a contest afar off—it is now going on. It is no mere war of words—it is a war of principles—it is a war between civil and religious liberty and the Papal Hierarchy; in which, if we but maintain our principles, we are certain of victory; but in which, if we yield any ground, we shall be defeated. What, then, is to be our attitude? That Christianity which presided over the framing of our political institutions, which accorded Christian toleration to all men, with the right of private judgment, in the very teeth of Papal dogmas; that Christianity which pervaded and still pervades our common law and our legislation, must be upheld, defended, propagated, taught to the old and to the young. If that Christianity which our fathers received, and under the light of which they framed our laws and institutions, is not to be an active, positive, pervading religion, then it must perish, and toleration with it. It is our system of Christianity which enjoins toleration; Papal Christianity forbids it, and brands it as the right of heresy. Can ours, as some contend, be a negative system, retreating before every claim of a right of conscience? The other, it is now seen, is an active, progressive system, using its right of conscience as a weapon to secure its advancing movements There is then a clear duty resting upon all that host of Americans who hold the great American principle of Christian toleration, and that is, to continue their system of Christianity as the one appropriate to the country and its institutions, and as the only system in which civil and religious liberty can long survive.

Protestantism does not lack vigor in its members; but here an occasion arises in which it must exercise some energy both in brain and body. It must move in solid mass against the enemy of Christian toleration. It cannot shrink from the struggle without betraying its dearest interests and ultimate safety. Energy and firmness will ensure a quiet and long reign — a permanent conquest. One false step now, may never be retrieved. Let those who would sustain our tolerant system of Christianity, feel that conscience compels them to sustain it; that they must sustain it, or prove recreant to their own convictions of duty. Let them advance the claims of their system of Christianity with as much confidence and as much perseverance as they would their own personal rights. Let them study well the wide scope of constitutional limits within which these claims can be put forward. And having once ascertained their true path, let them maintain it, advancing with the progress of the age, and adhering firmly to American principles, civil and religious.

The mass of the Catholics in the United States neither entertain such views, nor suppose that their Priests entertain them. The mass of Protestants are as little aware that such odious principles are held by Romish ecclesiastics. If they were made sure of this, it would be difficult for the whole power of the public authorities to prevent their being driven from the country as its worst enemies.

There may be many Papal ecclesiastics in this country, as the mass of the laymen undoubtedly do, who regard these anti-American features of their system with distrust, if not aversion. There are many of whom we should have hoped better, had their names not been appended to the *imprimatur;* and especially is it hard to credit that the Bishop of New York holds any such doctrines as those so boldly advanced by Mr. Brownson : we think they are inconsistent with much that he has said and written. The sentiments and spirit of the author of "A Lecture on the importance of a Christian Basis for the Science of Political Economy," and of another on "The mixture of Civil and Ecclesiastical Power in the Government of the Middle Ages," seem of a very different tenor and spirit from those which pervade the pages of the Review and several other leading Papal periodicals. But whilst there may be many Romish Priests not holding opinions so inconsistent with our American institutions, it must be remembered that such individuals do not govern the Papal Church. *It* holds no such liberal opinions; it makes no compromises; its object is ever the same, the absorption of all power, temporal and spiritual; and its general policy, however it may vary, is ever directed towards that end. There may be every variety of ambition among these ecclesiastics, from that which is not censurable, to that which pursues, with untiring eagerness, the grand object; yet there can be no general deviation from this one design. This is no harsh judgment, though it may appear so to such of the Papal Ecclesiastics as are not conscious of such claims on the part of their Church. The great features of the Papacy are, its claim to be THE CHURCH, out of whose pale, no salvation is possible. The claim of an infallible Pope carries Papal Ecclesiastics, by a direct path, into the policy we have ascribed to them. If they believe men can only be saved but in their Church, it ceases to be violence, it is charity, to "compel them to come" within her communion : if men refuse to accept the Papal offer of salvation, and resist her violent measures or ridicule her pretensions, it is a mercy to persecute and destroy them, that others may be deterred from following the dangerous example. It is impossible for men holding such a doctrine, to refrain from employing every practicable means to enlarge their authority. They have the double inducement — the love of power natural to all men, and the belief that they are doing God service. They aim at dominion, not only for dominion's sake, but to increase the number of saints. It is but justice to say, however, that the present race of Romish ecclesiastics are not responsible for the monstrous system of spiritual domination which they uphold. They have been trained from their earliest youth to the positions they now occupy. It would be contrary to any just estimate of human nature, to expect them to see clearly, or reject its enormities. Their conduct is just what we might expect from men thus educated. Our quarrel is not with the men, but with the system.

There may be Bishops and Priests who suppose that the spiritual and temporal power towards which their Church proceeds with such a determined step, would not be abused; they commit the mistake of not seeing that all power in human hands is certain to be abused, but most of all, that which has no assignable limit; and that is the nature of the power which their Church claims. She claims it because she is infallible, and does not fear to wield it because she is infallible. But man is fallible, and all the agents of the Church are fallible, and the greater power she wields, the more mischief is committed. The Church of Rome has always abused her power, and so has every other church. If any lesson is plainly taught in history, it is that power temporal or spiritual is no proper accompaniment of Christianity, which needs no other than the power of truth and persuasion.

This grasping for power is not confined to the Papal Church, though displayed most conspicuously there. The history of Protestantism furnishes striking examples. It is seen in all the established churches, and can be detected in every denomination. It is to be remarked that it is not always the intelligence or piety of a church which determines or shapes its policy, but the active intervention of men who attempt to distinguish themselves by peculiar zeal, to procure place, or patronage, or notoriety, by pushing themselves into conspicuous positions, by assuming superiority, by advancing new claims upon denominational loyalty, and by intensifying every expression and every feature of their denomination.

The more inactive members of a church cannot afford to be outdone by these special zealots, and so they suffer themselves to be carried wherever the more active and zealous ride the denominational hobby. They may disapprove, but they either lack courage or energy to say so, and the reins are thus surrendered to interested, unworthy, mistaken, or unskilful hands. It is power abused. The only safety for the Church of Christ is, to assume no powers, and then none will be abused. In every large denomination of Christians there will be found strong tendencies towards the formation of governing cliques, and towards the centralization of power: a few men in central positions often make their influence felt to the circumference, and mould measures and men to their liking. As soon as this power is seen to be concentrated in a few hands, a host, who hope to avail themselves of it in some way, show ready court, and hasten to propitiate and strengthen a power which may either render them a service, or do them an injury. Power, both civil and religious, always struggles to enlarge itself, and often from motives wholly unexceptionable. There is no doubt that power, both in Church and State, increases the opportunities of doing good; but let it be remembered, power corrupts the heart and increases the facilities of committing evil. The Papacy, then, is built upon a system destined to certain corruption, and to the commission of vast mischief. It is a system of centralization: it is a system which, in its nature, begets ambition, lust of power, and usurpation, and these bring forth those vices of deeper dye which blacken the calender of human crime.

The finger of history has written this upon every century of the Papal Hierarchy, in terms to which no denial can be offered, and which shows, that whatever may have been the piety of the people, scarcely a semblance of Christianity existed among the leaders of those who professed to be the lineal successors of the Apostles. It seems almost impossible for the thoughtful Christian, whether Catholic or Protestant, not to see that the Papal Hierarchy is a system at war with Christianity, and with every form of authority and every kind of government that does not bow to its wishes. It undermines and weakens every other form of power, and then sinks by its own corruptions. It is purer and more unexceptionable in its manifestations here than elsewhere, only because it has not yet obtained power enough to work its own ruin. The separation between Catholics and their spiritual governors is not wider than facts warrant. There is very little in common between the Catholics of this country and their Priests and Bishops. The latter being placed over them, and removed from them without their consent, real sympathy between pastor and people is seldom maintained. All other Christians in this country select their own spiritual teachers. This is not only denied to Catholics, but they are not even permitted to own or manage their own churches, church-yards, or cemeteries. They are denied all participation in the councils of the Church; they are neither represented nor heard in the assemblies in which questions of grave import to their religious welfare are decided. Submission is their chief duty; submission of mind, of body, and of purse. When the head is infallible, the other members must obey.

It is very visible, even on the surface, that there is a struggle going on between the free spirit engendered among the Catholics by our American institutions and the Hierarchy of Rome. There has, for years, been an effort on the part of the people to retain the management of their own church property. Their claim has never received the least favor. The indignity put upon our Catholic fellow-citizens is doubtless more felt and talked of, than has yet been made public. The Hierarchy believe that their system is strong enough to overcome this disposition, and to struggle successfully with American freedom. That will prove a fatal mistake. In other things, the Hierarchy show themselves unequal to the new position in which they are placed here; they should comprehend it better before adopting their final policy. The Papacy of Europe cannot succeed here. It has had a continual struggle for existence there; the attempt to carry out its principles has been steadily resisted. It is hastening to a collision with our free institutions which cannot be very remote; concealing within its bosom discontent and a sense of wrong, in the day of struggle between toleration and liberty on the one hand, and spiritual domination on the other, these will burst forth to the confusion and defeat of the power which has so long smothered them. It strikes us forcibly, that a profound knowledge of human nature, in which the members of the Hierarchy, above all other men, ought to be versed, should teach them that their system cannot eventually triumph in the United States. They should be able to see that either the American system of civil and religious liberty must be modified, or their system, opposed in its theory and results to both, must undergo change. They can move in harmony only whilst the Hierarchy is too weak to inflict injury. Its success heretofore is owing to its inability to betray itself. Its inherent power of progress is very great, whilst under wholesome restraint, and whilst prevented from exhibiting its despotic character. We regard a collision between the free institutions of this country and the Papal Hierarchy to be as certain, as that liberty to worship God according to the dictates of each man's conscience, the main religious feature of these free institutions, is opposed to the Papal dogma that there is, and can be, no true worship of God out of that church; to be just as certain, as that religious toleration and religious intolerance are irreconcilable. The ultimate result of this struggle need not be feared; though deplorable events might be apprehended in its progress, if the Catholic laity were disposed to sustain the Priesthood. This they will never do, when the designs of the Hierarchy are laid bare, for they are really Americans, and neither seek nor desire any radical change in our political system.

The worldly wisdom of the Hierarchy fails in the circumstances in which it is placed here. It does not appreciate its position nor its difficulties, and, unless checked, it is pushing on to the greatest disasters it has encountered since the Reformation, the most damaging exposures, and the most signal defeat. The history of Catholicism in this country reveals some facts which many Protestants did not anticipate. The Catholic religion can live and flourish in the face of an open Bible, free institutions, general intelligence, and general education. This result no doubt surprises the Hierarchy as much as it does many Protestants; but this result is pregnant with lessons which the Hierarchy is slow to learn. Their minds are moulded after the Italian or Old World fashion; they know that an open Bible and liberty of worship would drive all the Priests out of the Papal dominions in a fortnight, and they cannot understand why it is not so here. That is a problem demanding their profoundest study. Why do they discourage the reading of the Bible here, when their very opposition induces many to read it who would not otherwise think of it? Why do they prohibit it to the children in the schools, when these children mingle freely with others who are familiar with it, and grow up with them in terms of intimacy; when Bibles are met at every turn — in every hotel, in every vessel, and when, to a curiosity piqued by prohibition, men add the striking results produced upon Protestants by their devotion to it? That the more active and energetic minds among the Catholics read the Bible, cannot be doubted, and the reading has not produced any general defection from Catholic ranks. Many persons, in fact, perfectly familiar with the Bible, trained to its study from infancy, have left Protestantism and become Catholics, and many of these are the men who now place the claims of the Hierarchy on the highest ground. It is perfectly plain then, for facts have demonstrated it, that the Catholic religion can live and prosper with free schools and the Bible in them.

This fact, and numberless others which must, at times, attract their notice, should suggest to the Hierarchy the propriety and necessity of establishing an American Church — the Catholic Church of the United States. There have been many organizations of portions of the Catholic Church in a greater or less degree of dependence on the Holy See. The Papal Church has always been in hot water between her attempts to take care of nations, kings, emperors, and people, and the foolish aversion of these to acknowledge the rights of the Church, and to submit their affairs to the control of the Papacy. Mr. Brownson complains of this European stubbornness which every where, in times past, and every where now, resists this maternal authority, and prevents the whole world from being happy and peaceful in the bosom of the Church. There is not a country in the world more quiet at this moment under Papal drilling than our own. It is, therefore, a fit time to form a Catholic Church for this country, in harmony with its principles and its institutions. In no other way can ultimate collision be escaped. The two great systems cannot prosper long side by side. The older having come to dwell with the younger, must make the needful concession. The Gallican Church was a concession. But something better than that is required here. It is but simple good policy to give the management of all church property to the people of each congregation: there must be some among them sufficiently faithful and sufficiently intelligent. It is but like good policy to let the people have some voice in the choice and dismissal of their pastors, and so much is required to place Catholics on an equality with the freemen around them. The subordination to Rome has been, in most European countries, for several centuries, very slight indeed: in this country it should be less than in the least, and be confined, of course, to questions purely theological, and be only exercised when invoked by American ecclesiastics.

But above all, and in this lies the chief argument for the change from the European to the American system, the Catholic Priesthood should unite in some great public act, framed in open assembly, avowing their hearty adoption of the principle of religious toleration, as announced in the constitutions of the various States of the Union, and admitting that all truly pious persons may be saved, by whatever name they may be called. Measures like these would give the Catholic Church a security in this country equal to the stability of the country itself, and insure it a higher destiny than its warmest friends should hope for at present. Its struggle then with other churches would be a struggle for truth, not for power. In our view, this would save the people of the United States from one of the most troublesome convulsions which now threatens their future peace.

Advice is always esteemed a cheap commodity, though it may cost the adviser very dear. In the present case it is not intended to be insulting. The truth is, the very great frankness of Mr. Brownson is infectious, and the openness of his heart requires something equally frank in return.

We confess ourselves indebted to him in many respects, and we heartily wish that his bold denunciations of Protestantism were read by all in the United States who are capable of profiting by such lessons. His sketch is a broad caricature, but he puts in at times a lineament so true that it must bring a tinge of shame on every Protestant face that sees it. He draws a picture of the Papacy so ideal, so purely imaginative, so grand, so unlike any thing above, or below, or on the earth, that he may safely be left to worship it as the image of "nothing in Heaven above or on the earth beneath, or in the waters under the earth."

APPENDIX B.

We transfer from the Appendix of "Politics for American Christians," the following remarks, which appear appropriate to the topic we have been considering.

"It is a sad mistake to assume that the field of humanity has all been explored, or that the heights or the depths of Christianity have been reached as yet by any human eye. The landscape in each widens as we advance, and no human glance can ever cover the whole. But no eye should be satisfied while more remains to be seen. It requires no small effort to detach one's self from the busy turmoil and exciting scenes of social and religious life, and to withdraw so far as to look from a place apart at the drama enacted upon the stage of life. The spectacle thus obtained is worthy the highest intellectual effort; it is instructive beyond all definite estimation.

Let any one who would find this point of view, ascertain what *all of Protestantism* is doing in the cause of humanity; how it is promoting the progress of social amelioration; and the position it occupies on all the great questions which most concern the peace, and happiness, and well-being of men in this life. It may cost many years of effort and inquiry to occupy a position which will afford a full view of the subject, the complications of which are enough to deter any but the most resolute. It cannot be done without severe mental discipline and painful struggles; for many things have to be unlearned. But it costs no sacrifice of orthodoxy. On the contrary, it would vindicate orthodoxy from much for which it should never have been responsible; it will afford a clearer view of the elementary doctrines of Christianity than can be had in any other way. This view must be obtained with one hand toward Divinity, the other toward Humanity, an open Bible before the eyes, a heart raised to God for the enlightening influences of his Holy Spirit, and with a devout looking, not only to Christ our atoning Saviour, but to Christ our Lawgiver, our Teacher, our Great Examplar, not less to be *heeded* and *obeyed* than to be accepted and worshipped. This method of inquiry will exalt Christianity above all former estimation, by exhibiting its fitness and applicability, not only to save men in eternity, but to save them from a vast sum of misery, wickedness, and oppression in this world; thus increasing their grounds for gratitude to God, and leaving them time and opportunity to prepare for Heaven.

Has collective Protestantism no grave faults to answer for? Does it claim infallibility? If not, if it be conceded that Protestantism has failings, then what are they? Are they sins of omission or commission, or both? Let a deep search be made into the grand household and conscience of Protestantism. Let there be no flinching, and no sparing; let neither spiritual pride nor false shame prevent a full discovery and an honest confession. Whilst Protestantism is dear to all for the good done under its banners, and for that which is still doing, let no one identify it with Christianity, and thus make the latter responsible for all that passes under the name of the former. The sins of the purest Christian are still sins, and make no part of his Christianity; they are to be sought for, and repented of, and avoided. So neither should the sins of Protestantism be excused or covered, much less should they be allowed to bring reproach upon the cause of Christ. One of the great sins of Protestantism is, the refusal to co-operate — to be, even for the advancement of the Redeemer's kingdom, a unit; even for the common defence against a common enemy. Christianity has one voice, and utters simply the teachings of the Holy Scriptures; Protestantism has many tongues, and utters, in the interpretation of the Scriptures, a variety of voices, and these very far from being in harmony. Yet let the inquiry be made, if there be not points of concord, and those of vital import to the highest interests of Christianity and humanity, on which Protestantism can speak with one voice, and work with undivided energies. If there be such points of concord, admitting unity of voice and action, and no advantage taken of them, then Protestantism is guilty of a great and deadly offence against Christianity.

Let any Christian man, any real friend of humanity, carefully and continuously survey the actual condition of the human family, in its various phases of barbarism and civilization; in its aspects of happiness and suffering; in its social and political institutions; in its relations with labor, with capital, with commerce; let him consider the nature of the progress which he observes, and the tendencies which are at work; let him note all the hopes and promises which can be gathered from every form of monarchy, aristocracy, and democracy, and from every conceivable combination of them which human ingenuity can devise; and from every form of philososophy, and every project of reform; let him superadd, from the page of history, all that man has done for man in the most favorable circumstances, and finally, let him sum up that which is hopeful in human prospects, not forgetting that some of the most boasted human triumphs have been purchased by the direst human calamities, that the tendencies to evil do not lessen in proportion to the increase of intelligence, while the power of mischief enlarges; and he must be convinced that there is no inherent virtue, no moral power, no good inclinations in man, adequate to such a social and political regeneration of society as appears to be attainable by a creature of his faculties and endowments. Such a survey must convince the observer that no such moral power exists, except in the influences of Christianity, to which he is forced to attribute the largest share of the actual progress made in human welfare since the Christian era. In this survey, the first great feature is, that, during the early ages of Christianity, its moral power to renovate human society and promote human happiness was plainly demonstrated to the world; the highest earthly hopes of man were placed within the reach of Christian effort. The early history of Christianity appeared to promise a bright day for the human family; but human depravity and perversity triumphed in that struggle; Christianity degenerated into Romanism, and the evening of that bright dawn ended in the long night of the Middle Ages. Thus the first experiment of Christianity, regarded as the only power adequate to secure the highest earthly happiness, failed signally in Papal hands. The Reformation was the era of another experiment, which has now been three centuries in progress. This time, the administration of Christianity is divided between Romanism, whose evil tendencies are as great as heretofore, and Protestantism, which has assumed a position of scarcely less power, and perhaps greater influence. Protestantism is now, and has, during its whole history, been regarded as the worthiest representative of Christianity. The purest individual Christian laments his insufficiency and utter unworthiness, and yet how far is such an one above the collective piety of Protestantism, split, as it is, into shapeless and countless fragments, hostile factions swelling with incessant intestinal broils and explosions. How imperfect a representation of the holy cause it impersonates! It presents a foundation of heaving, shifting sands, upon which to build the fabric of human welfare, rather than one "of rock which cannot be shaken." Must this experiment fail, and prove that Protestantism is also unequal to the task of applying Christianity to the earthly exigencies of humanity? For anything that the collective power and influence of Protestantism is now doing to promote national welfare or social reform, it may be apprehended that, at no distant period, the Protestant administration of Christianity will be subjected, not to a deep night of ignorance — that is no longer possible — but to a long day of superlative intelligence, crime, and misery.

Christianity is a system of man's duty to God and to his fellowmen. It enjoins all that is included in love to God, and all that is included in kindness to men. Its administration is, however, committed to men, and partakes in its every manifestation of human infirmity. And while it offers much that is beautiful, it reveals more that is grievous and shocking. Christianity involves, wherever there is liberty of speech and action, a variety of opinions and interpretations, and consequently a variety of churches or sects, various organizations and forms of ecclesiastical government; also creeds, confessions, articles, liturgies, forms of worship, a ministry — divinely appointed, or religiously instituted; assemblies for worship, houses or churches in which to worship, and church architecture.

Upon all these, and many more like things, there prevails, among even Protestant Christians, wide and apparently irreconcilable differences of opinion. These differences naturally magnify the objects to which they relate, in the minds of those who permit themselves to dwell upon them, and thus men's minds are seduced into merely collateral channels. Their whole time and their whole minds become absorbed in minor matters, while they suffer the substance to slip from their attention and sink from their sight. It is not necessary to weigh the exact value of these externals of Christianity, in their true place, and order, and use, but it is easy to say that they are of no use if abused or misapplied, and that they become a positive evil when they are substituted for Christianity itself, as is largely the case. None of these things, at the best, are to be received as Christianity, neither is it to be held responsible for any abuse of them. It is as high above all these externals as heaven is above the earth. If our faith be too weak, and our energies insufficient to exemplify Christianity in our lives, we should not permit our conception to fall as low as our practice. We can never rise in our exemplification, if our conception be inadequate and unworthy. If men find it hard to act beyond the line of denominational boundaries, let not their faith suffer by assuming a narrower scope for Christianity itself than the most enlarged views their minds are capable of grasping. Its grandest aspect is that in which it not only offers eternal life and happiness to lost men, but wins their consent to the message of mercy by offering all that man can do and feel for man, as earnest of the authenticity and verity of the message. It is that in which, while it points to men the way to Heaven, smooths their path through this world to the utmost extent which human love and sympathy can go, thus furnishing the nearest approximation which can be made in this world, to the life of love in the world to come. It is a grand feature in Christianity, that its simple but comprehensive principles and injunctions involve the very elements of social life, the utmost duty of man to man. "Thou shalt love thy neighbour as thyself," is a command which reaches to the whole compass of human duty; we owe to our neighbor not merely alms, when he is poor; we ought to save him from becoming poor. We owe him a better position in society; we owe him every social advantage — good laws, good institutions, a good government, a happy and prosperous country. What we owe to one we owe to all, and all in like manner owe to us.

These obligations no human being can fulfil, under the requirements of the gospel, short of expending his whole energies and his whole opportunities. But the advantage of our neighbor is not to be found only in the bounds of his own country; it must be sought in the happiest relations of his own country with all the nations of the world; peace with all nations, and interchange of every good office with all. This vast scope of human duty involves necessarily the study of all the themes involved in so wide a compass of human action — it involves the consideration of all that concerns human welfare in this world, in connection with its highest destiny in the next world. While, therefore, nothing is omitted in the sphere of immediate duties, there should be no failure to follow out all obligations to their largest consequences, and to widen the range of duty to the utmost range of mental power; extending the range of action and influence in proportion as the field of vision is enlarged. Very many, it is well known, have no faith in moral or social progress; they regard all speculations in reference to social amelioration, as, at the best, mere visionary dreams, if not what is far worse, downright socialism. But let no friend of the human family be deterred from any research, or inquiry, or speculation, looking to human advantage, by such narrowness of mind. Let him take the Gospels in his hand, and the light of all the other Scriptures, and he may go as far as his intelligence and knowledge of the world will carry him; and if he cannot secure the co-operation or approval of the Christian men of the present day, he will have the full sympathy of those who, having gone before, are observing the world from a point of view where nothing clouds their vision."

THE END.

www.ingramcontent.com/pod-product-compliance
Lightning Source LLC
LaVergne TN
LVHW011236110826
845150LV00006B/1648

* 9 7 8 1 4 2 5 5 1 3 9 3 1 *